THE COMPLETE GUIDE TO

Cross Training

THE COMPLETE GUIDE TO

Cross Training

Fiona Hayes

A & C Black • London

First published 1998 by
A & C Black (Publishers) Ltd
35 Bedford Row, London WC1R 4JH

ISBN 0 7136 4883 X

A CIP catalogue record for this book
is available from the British Library.

Acknowledgements
Cover photograph courtesy of Jump, Hamburg.
Diagrams on pages 4, 6, 8, 22, 38, 41, 46, 47, 49, 53, 68,
106, 109, 120, 121, 142, 143, 146 by
Ron Dixon of 1–11 line-art.

Typeset in 10½ on 12pt Palatino

Printed and bound in Great Britain by
Biddles Ltd, Guildford and Kings Lynn

Contents

Acknowledgements

I would like to thank my daughters, Rhian and Frances, who made sure I remembered to eat while I wrote this book.

I would also like to thank Jonathan Taylor of A & C Black for being so helpful and patient.

Mostly I would like to thank Tony Lycholat for his support and guidance, and for the time he spent discussing detail with me and reading through my material to check technical accuracy.

Finally I would like to thank all my personal training clients for all that I have learned from them.

Dedication

Quiet, funny, gentle
That is how I remember you

I remember running on the beach
so fast my feet were left behind,
holding your hand, flying;
sand in my hair.

I remember swimming,
riding through the waves
on your broad strong back
safe and happy.

You gave to me the love of movement
This book is for you.
Thank you Dad.

List of abbreviations

- ACSM = American College of Sports Medicine
- Acta Med Scand. = *Acta Medica Scandinavica*
- Acta Physiol Scand. = *Acta Physiologica Scandinavica*
- Am. J. Sports Med. = *American Journal of Sports Medicine*
- Can. J. Appl. Physiol. = *Canadian Journal of Applied Physiology*
- Eur. J. Appl. Physiol. Occup. Physiol. = *European Journal of Applied Physiology and Occupational Physiology*
- GSSE = Gatorade Sports Science Exchange
- IHRSA = International Health and Racquet Sportsclub Association
- J. Appl. Physiol. = *Journal of Applied Physiology*
- Med. Sci. Sport and Exerc. = *Medical Science in Sport and Exercise*
- Med. Sci. Sport and Exerc. Suppl. = *Medical Science in Sport and Exercise Supplement*
- Res. Q. Exerc. Sport. = *Research Quarterly for Exercise and Sport*
- Sports Med. = *Sports Medicine*

About Cross Training

Chapter 1

What is Cross Training?

QUOTE

'When individuals successfully meet the challenge of exercise during the preparation for and participation in sport, they do so as a result of an exquisitely orchestrated collection of physiological and metabolic events.'
PROFESSOR CLYDE WILLIAMS

Whether training for general fitness and health or for sports performance this is true. The body is a fascinating machine, beautiful in its complexity. It is a machine in which not only physiological and metabolic events interact, but in which psychological aspects such as motivation and mental attitude play an

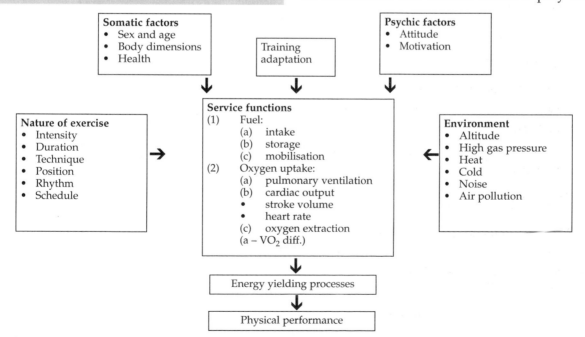

Somatic factors
- Sex and age
- Body dimensions
- Health

Training adaptation

Psychic factors
- Attitude
- Motivation

Nature of exercise
- Intensity
- Duration
- Technique
- Position
- Rhythm
- Schedule

Service functions
(1)   Fuel:
    (a)   intake
    (b)   storage
    (c)   mobilisation
(2)   Oxygen uptake:
    (a)   pulmonary ventilation
    (b)   cardiac output
    •   stroke volume
    •   heart rate
    (c)   oxygen extraction
    $(a - VO_2 \text{ diff.})$

Environment
- Altitude
- High gas pressure
- Heat
- Cold
- Noise
- Air pollution

Energy yielding processes

Physical performance

Figure 1.1 Factors influencing aerobic activity (Taken from *Textbook of Work Physiology* (third edition) by Per Olaf Astrand and Kaare Rodahl (McGraw-Hill))

important role in influencing outcomes, whether that be high-level performance, or simply the motivation to move.

However, this 'exquisitely orchestrated collection of physiological and metabolic events' can 'get out of tune'.

In order to play the perfect symphony our training must be geared to making the most of all the aspects of fitness. Therefore, to cross train effectively we must first understand at least a little about the orchestra and how its different sections play together.

Figure 1.1 on page 1 illustrates the various influences that affect physical performance. Some of these influences are beyond our control. For instance, somatic factors such as body dimensions play a role in determining the sports that we may be good at. In the same way that jockeys are small, international oarsmen are all well over six feet tall. Long levers are needed in the mechanics of rowing. If you are not over six feet the chances of you becoming a world class oarsman are minimal.

Even the response to training is different in different people and is genetically determined. It is well known that top class endurance athletes have a genetic advantage in that they are born with higher than average ability to utilise oxygen. World class bodybuilders start with a fairly symmetrical shape, broad shoulders and narrow hips, but have the genetic ability to build muscle. Genetics determines our ceiling of ability. Whether or not we reach the ceiling is determined by how we train.

How we train as well as how much we train gives us control over some of the factors influencing performance; that is, those factors that can be trained, such as strength, endurance, flexibility and motor skills (e.g. speed, reaction time, balance). These adaptations to training, while having a genetic ceiling, are nevertheless influenced by what we do in training. From being untrained, everyone – no matter who they are – can improve their ability to take in and

> ### DEFINITION
>
> **Maximum oxygen uptake** or VO_2max (also known as aerobic capacity or cardio-respiratory endurance capacity) is the highest amount of oxygen that the body can consume for the aerobic production of ATP; that is, the amount of oxygen that the body can take in and utilise in the working muscles for the production of energy. VO_2max may be measured by a maximal test or estimated from the results of sub-maximal tests.

utilise oxygen (VO_2max) by exercising regularly. Everyone can also improve their strength by exercising regularly, but even the genetically gifted have to train if they want to make the most of their talents.

The 'exquisitely orchestrated' sequence of events is a combination of muscular contraction for strength, power and endurance, mechanical events, plus intake, storage and usage of fuel to power muscular contraction. So complex is the body that it reacts to different training stimuli in different ways, even to the extent that the order in which we arrange the exercises in a strength workout may change the body's reaction to that workout, and the intensity with which we start a training session can affect the fuel we utilise for the whole workout.

In order to write a symphony you must be able to write scores for a whole orchestra of different instruments in such a way that each individual piece blends into the whole. In order to write a training programme the same is true. You must understand how to blend training for strength, power, speed, skill and endurance. You must know about the fuels of performance, the psychology of training, and the importance of rest. Cross training makes this both easier and more difficult: easier in that different disciplines throw different aspects of training automatically into the pot, and more difficult in that for multi-sport athletes there are more disciplines in which all these aspects must be trained.

For the coach, then, cross training makes life both simple and fascinatingly complex.

For the sportsperson, whether you train for performance or for general fitness, cross training is good for your health.

♦ What is cross training? ♦

Cross training is a long term exercise programme made up of different activities and sports in order to provide variety and reduce the risk of injury while improving all-round fitness.

A cross training programme may include competitive sports, outdoor activities such as climbing, walking, cycling, kayaking and canoeing, and fitness activities such as weight training and aerobics.

The appeal of cross training is in the variety of exercise in the programme, which serves to maintain long term interest and tax different muscle groups in different ways. Thus one day the participant may run, putting greater stress on the muscles and joints of the legs, and the next day swim, reducing the impact on the joints and working the upper body.

QUOTE

'Everyone has limits on the time they can devote to exercise, and cross training simply gives you the best return on your investment. Balanced fitness with minimum injury risk and maximum fun.'
TOP TRIATHLETE PAULA NEWBY-FRASER

If the cross training programme is put together well, this type of training readily accommodates the multi-activity person who wishes to compete in more than one discipline.

INTEREST

The appeal of cross training

Cross training has become a buzz word in fitness training circles. Its rise in popularity is reflected by the number of cross training shoes and instructor training programmes now available.

Gym-based cross training competitions involving a variety of tests based on cardiovascular and resistance machines are becoming increasingly popular as inter- and intra-club challenges.

The boom in triathlon (swim, bike, run competitions) has spread and lead to an increase in competition that accommodates multi-sport participants. Biathlon involves swim and run, and duathlon involves bike and run. These competitions are now advertised in popular running, cycling and fitness magazines and include a number of distances to accommodate all levels from beginner to seasoned athlete. Further variety is provided by changing the bike leg, traditionally a road time trial section, to a mountain bike section, or changing the run from a road run to a cross-country run. In some events a kayak or sailing section is included either as well as, or instead of, the swim.

Also increasing in popularity is adventure racing, involving outdoor activities such as fell running, walking, climbing, kayaking, skiing, mountain biking and horse riding: competitive cross training for the outdoor enthusiast and survival specialist.

◆ Balanced fitness ◆

Physical fitness is the integration and balance of a variety of components affecting the cardio-vascular and pulmonary systems (the heart and lungs), the skeleton and joints, the muscles, and the nervous system.

To obtain all-round fitness, all aspects of fitness must be trained.

PHYSICAL FITNESS
is made up of

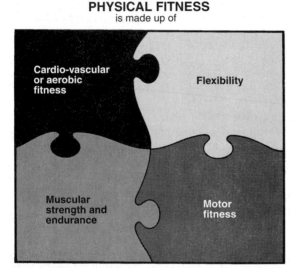

Figure 1.2 Physical fitness

◆ Why is training good for ◆ my heart and lungs?

Cardio-vascular fitness refers to the condition of the heart and circulatory system. Training that is endurance-based such as walking, running, swimming, rowing, canoeing, skating, skipping and dancing affect the heart, increasing its size, strength and function such that there is an increase in **stroke volume** and **cardiac output**. That is, more blood is pumped out of the heart at every single beat. This has the effect of reducing the pulse rate both at rest and at various intensities of exercise.

DEFINITION

- **Stroke volume** is the amount of blood ejected from the left ventricle of the heart during contraction.
- **Cardiac output** is the volume of blood pumped out by the heart per minute and is the stroke volume x the heart rate.

Therefore, at any given intensity the heart beats more slowly in a trained than in an untrained individual, and during exhaustive exercise the cardiac output is greater in the trained than in the untrained individual. This greater cardiac output is often attributed to the increase in size of the heart. In reality the increase in size is minimal and the increased cardiac output is largely the result of greater filling of the ventricles which results in a greater stroke volume.

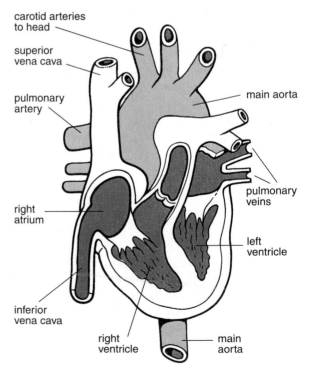

Figure 1.3 The heart

FACT

Blood carries:

- oxygen
- foodstuffs
- enzymes
- heat
- hormones
- waste products.

With the right type of training, improvements in the functioning of the heart are accompanied by improvements to general circulation – the blood transport system. There is an increase in the size and number of **capillaries** flowing through the regularly worked muscles. This allows the body to transport oxygen, nutrients, **hormones** and **enzymes** to the muscles, and waste products away from the muscles, more effectively.

DEFINITION

- **Capillaries** are small blood vessels forming a network throughout the body.
- **Hormones** are chemical messengers produced by the body and transported in the blood to the target tissue.
- **Enzymes** are complex proteins formed in living cells which assist chemical processes without being changed themselves, i.e. organic catalysts.

Blood pressure is the pressure that the blood exerts on the walls of the blood vessels. Thus an increase in the size and number of capillaries will decrease blood pressure both at rest and at work. Blood pressure at rest and during sub-maximal exercise decreases as a result of regular aerobic training.

FACT

Blood pressure is recorded using two numbers, e.g. 140/90. The larger number is systolic blood pressure, or the pressure during systole when the heart is contracting. The smaller number is diastolic blood pressure, or the pressure during diastole when the heart is relaxing. Normal blood pressure is often quoted as 120/80, though a range from 110/60 to 140/90 is usually accepted as normal. If blood pressure is consistently above 160/90 you should consult your doctor.[1]

Oxygen is carried in the blood in association with **haemoglobin**, a protein pigment containing iron which is found in red blood cells. Every haemoglobin molecule can carry four oxygen molecules. When the oxygen reaches the muscle it is given up by the haemoglobin and diffuses across the cell membranes and into the muscle where it is carried on another protein pigment called **myoglobin**.

DEFINITION

- **Haemoglobin** is the iron-containing pigment of red blood cells that carries oxygen in the blood.
- **Myoglobin** is a pigment found in muscle that transports oxygen from the cell membrane to the mitochondria.

Endurance training causes an increase in total blood volume and also in total haemoglobin levels in the blood. This improves the oxygen-carrying capacity of the blood. There is also an increase in the myoglobin content of the working muscle.

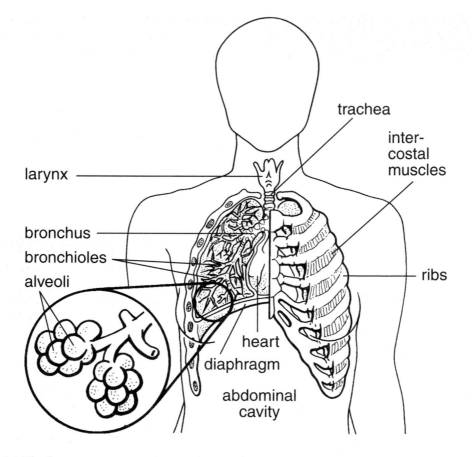

trachea

inter-
costal
muscles

larynx

bronchus

bronchioles

alveoli

ribs

heart

diaphragm

abdominal
cavity

Figure 1.4 The lungs

The lungs are the site of gaseous exchange; oxygen enters the bloodstream from the air, and carbon dioxide, a bi-product of the aerobic energy system, leaves the blood and is released back into the air. Regular endurance training improves the function of the lungs, by increasing the power and endurance of the intercostal muscles and the diaphragm.

Breathing occurs when the lungs are inflated and deflated like bellows. This is controlled by the muscle of the diaphragm, found spanning the bottom of the rib cage, and the intercostal muscles found between the ribs. Endurance training improves the function of these muscles and is associated with an increase in breathing volume. This higher maximum ventilation is a result of increases in both breathing frequency and **tidal volume**.

DEFINITION

Tidal volume is the amount of air that is moved in or out of the lungs in one breath. Improvements to the functioning of the lungs include greater capilliarisation, that is an increase in the size and number of blood vessels in the lungs which increases the capacity for gaseous exchange.

♦ Why is training good ♦ for my muscles?

Regular training of any variety will improve the function of muscles. Muscles rarely work in isolation; they may be causing movement around a joint or joints, they may be stabilising the body position, or they may be checking movement at a joint in order to prevent injury. Whatever the job of the muscle in any particular movement or posture, both strength and endurance may be involved. Maximum strength is the ability of a muscle or group of muscles to overcome a resistance once. Endurance is the ability of a muscle or group of muscles to overcome a resistance for an extended period of time, i.e. more than once.

OPINION

An increase in both strength and endurance in the muscles may benefit **health** by accommodating safe lifting and maintaining the integrity of the joints during movement.

An increase in both strength and endurance in the muscles may benefit **sports performance** by increasing the total work capacity of the muscles either in terms of volume or intensity or both.

♦ Why is training good ♦ for my skeleton?

INTEREST

One in four women have fractures related to osteoporosis by the age of 60. This becomes one in two by the age of 70.[2]

The skeleton is made up of living tissue. If the skeleton is not worked it will become weak in the same way that unused muscle becomes weak; if the skeleton is subjected to force it will become stronger. However, even in terms of skeletal strength, training is specific. Only those parts of the skeleton subjected to force will become stronger, thus a runner may have strong bones in the legs and hips but may not have strong bones in the forearms and wrists, and a tennis player may have greater strength in the bones in the playing arm than in the non-playing arm.

DEFINITION

Osteoporosis is a medical condition often referred to as 'brittle bone disease' because the bones become fragile and in severe cases may fracture spontaneously. Although this disease mainly affects women, the number of men affected is growing.

Strong bones are vital to health. The widespread incidence of **osteoporosis** is believed to be at least in part due to long term lack of exercise. Other factors include diet, age, gender and genetics.

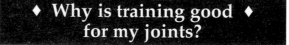

♦ Why is training good ♦ for my joints?

Wherever two or more bones meet there is a joint. Joints come in a variety of types but those most involved in movement are synovial joints. These joints allow for varying degrees of freedom of movement determined by the shape of the joint.

For instance, hinge joints such as the elbow allow for movement in one plane only, while ball and socket joints such as the hip allow for movement in three planes.

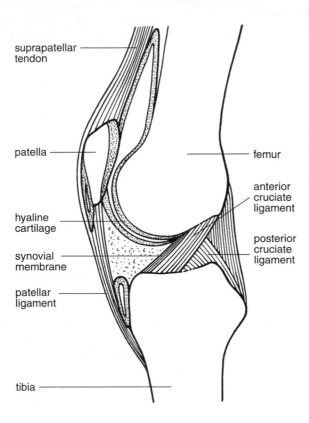

suprapatellar
tendon

patella

femur

hyaline
cartilage

anterior
cruciate
ligament

synovial
membrane

posterior
cruciate
ligament

patellar
ligament

tibia

Figure 1.5 Synovial joints: the knee

The ball and socket joint allows for a large range of movement in any one plane, while the joints in between each vertebrae of the spine allow for only a small range of movement.

Stabilising the joints are ligaments made up of connective tissue, and crossing the joints are muscles that effect the movement at the joint and increase stabilisation of the joint by holding the joint still or counteracting a movement.

Training may increase both the strength of the stabilising muscles and the strength of ligaments, thus maintaining the integrity of the joint during applications of force, such as when landing from a jump.

◆ Why is training good for ◆ my nervous system?

The nervous system is the control centre for the body. Any movement involves contracting individual muscle fibres or groups of muscle fibres in the right sequence. Simultaneously, opposing muscle fibres must be allowed to relax in order that they do not block that movement from happening. This is known as reciprocal innervation.

The nervous system controls the contraction and relaxation of muscle fibres and so is in charge of the combinations and sequences, both intra muscularly (within a muscle) and inter muscularly (between different muscles or groups of muscles). Learning the correct sequences of intra and inter muscular contraction to carry out a movement is the acquisition of skill, thus learning a physical skill involves training the nervous system. As the body tires, the nervous system also tires and skill is reduced. Training the body for endurance has the effect of increasing the endurance of the nervous system as well as increasing the endurance of muscles.

◆ Freedom of movement ◆

Ease of movement is accommodated by the joints and the muscles. Flexibility is joint specific, thus each individual joint or joint complex may perform differently. It is possible to have a good range of movement in the shoulder joints and a poor range of movement in the hips. Range of movement is affected by the shape of the joint, the connective tissues such as ligaments and joint capsules, and the muscles crossing the joint and the skin. As we age we tend to become less flexible. By continuing to be active and to train flexibility we can, however, reduce the loss in flexibility and maintain ease of movement. Flexibility training should therefore be an integral part of every training programme.

◆ How much training ◆ should I do?

This depends very much on what you wish to get out of your training. Do you simply want to be healthy, or do you want to compete at a sport? If your main aim is to improve your health or remain healthy then you need do far less training than if you play sport. If you wish to take part in some type of activity such as hill walking, climbing, sailing or wind surfing, even if you consider that activity to be fun rather than of a competitive nature, you will need to be fitter than if simply maintaining health.

Are there any recommended guidelines for fitness?

The American College of Sports Medicine issued guidelines for fitness that are widely accepted throughout the world. They state that the minimum activity levels for health are 30–60 minutes of moderate intensity aerobic activity, such as a brisk walk, on most days of the week.[3]

HEALTH	FITNESS	SPORT
30–60 mins of moderate intensity activity such as a brisk walk on most days of the week.	20 mins three times per week of aerobic activity at 50–90% VO$_2$max. Strength work twice a week, using one to two sets of eight to ten repetitions of eight to ten exercises covering the whole body.	Training should be specific. Training must allow you to peak for specific events.

Figure 1.6 Suggested guidelines for training

Physical Activity and Health, A Report of the Surgeon General[4] is widely used as a reference document and restates the ACSM guidelines.

QUOTE

'All people over the age of two years old should accumulate at least 30 minutes of endurance-type activity of at least moderate intensity on most, preferably all, days of the week. Additional health and functional benefits of physical activity can be achieved by adding more time in moderate intensity activity, or by substituting more vigorous intensity activity.'
REPORT OF THE SURGEON GENERAL

The report goes on to say that:

QUOTE

'Strength development activities (resistance training) should be performed at least twice per week. At least eight to 10 strength developing exercises that use the major muscle groups of the legs, trunk, arms and shoulders should be performed at each session, with one or two sets of eight to 12 repetitions of each exercise.'

Of course, following the guidelines on minimum levels of fitness for health will not equip you for sports performance. Thus to play sport we need to examine the demands of the sports and base fitness training on these demands.

♦ I run and train with weights. ♦ Why do I need to cross train as well?

If you run and weight train you are already cross training. Running works your cardio-vascular system and develops muscular endurance in the legs, while weight training works on muscular strength and endurance in your upper body. Thus your training programme may be more balanced than if you simply run or simply weight train. Most people who work out in gyms cross train using cardio-vascular machines such as treadmills, steppers, rowing machines and static bikes to improve their aerobic fitness, and use resistance equipment to work on muscular strength. Many people combine weights or resistance training indoors with walking, running or cycling outdoors to the same effect.

Combining different activities utilises different body parts and different combinations of muscles, even different combinations of muscle fibres within a muscle. This does not happen to the same extent in single activity training. Thus a more balanced fitness programme emerges.

♦ Cross training and health ♦

The well researched and documented health benefits associated with exercise are only apparent in those who exercise regularly and long term. Statistics show that most people who start an exercise programme drop out within the first three months.[5] Even in supervised exercise programmes the dropout rate is around 50%.[6] Cross training can provide variety which may prevent the boredom often associated with continuing an exercise programme.

Some people are put off exercise because they started training and picked up an injury. They have to stop doing their chosen activity so they give up exercising altogether.

♦ Cross training and sport ♦

Increased volume of training is associated with overuse injuries. This is due to the extra stress that repetitive movements place upon the musculoskeletal system. By changing the activity regularly and thus reducing the repetition of movement, cross training allows for the increased levels of fitness brought about by increases in training volume without a concomitant increase in the risk of injury.

Single sport participants often show imbalances of muscle strength, muscle mass and flexibility. For instance, the quadriceps muscles at the front of the thigh are often visibly larger on the dominant leg in squash players (i.e. the leg most commonly lunged on). Likewise, tennis players often have greater muscle mass in the playing arm than in the non-playing arm. These imbalances can lead to injury, however as cross training utilises different sports, imbalances are less likely to occur than in single activity participants.

♦ What if I become injured ♦ and can't train?

It may be that individual variations in joint configuration play a large part in risk of injury and that for some people the risk rises with increases in volumes of training. Many sportspeople who become injured simply give up exercise until their injury is better. This time of complete rest, while accommodating the recovery from the injury, sets back their training programme dramatically. A

INTEREST

A study of runners evaluated the increased risk of injury with respect to the:

- gender
- age
- obesity
- weekly mileage
- time per mile during training
- time and place of running
- stretching habits

of the participants.

It was concluded that only weekly mileage was positively associated with increased incidence of injury.[7]

cross training programme, because it uses different sports and therefore puts different stresses on the muscle and joint complexes, maintains fitness while the injury is healing.

INTEREST

A study showed that injuries in runners were related to increased weekly mileage and increased frequency of running or racing, and that runners who did not participate in any other sport were more likely to become injured.[8]

One of my personal training clients, unable to continue her sport of distance running while recovering from a stress fracture in her foot, maintained her cardio-vascular fitness and aerobic capacity by cycling and swimming. Only two weeks after she started to run again she ran a personal best in a 10km race.

Rehabilitation

Maintenance of fitness through cross training not only reduces the time spent reaching 'playing' fitness again after injury, but may speed up the healing process by reducing muscle loss, strengthening the injured area and correcting any muscular imbalances. While continuing to train, the stress on the injured area can gradually be increased as the injury heals and the new tissue becomes stronger or the joint becomes more stable.

♦ Is cross training beneficial ♦ for young athletes?

Most experts recommend that pre-pubescent children should participate in a variety of sports rather than specialising in one, even if a particular talent is discovered at an early age. Specialising too early may result in 'burn out' or in an overuse injury.

Injury prevention is particularly important in growing children, who should be supervised by a trained coach or instructor with specialist knowledge of coaching children. Careful monitoring of training will help protect against the possibility of serious injuries occurring to bone growth centres.

Cross training is therefore particularly suitable for young athletes.

1 The ACSM Guidelines for Exercise Testing and Prescription (4th edition)
2 The Osteoporosis Society
3 ACSM Guidelines (1995)
4 U.S. Department of Health and Human Services, Centers for Disease Control and Prevention, National Center for Chronic Disease Prevention and Health Promotion (1996)
5 IHRSA
6 Exercise Fitness and Health, a Consensus of Current Knowledge
7 Blair, S.N., Kohl, H.W. and Goodyear, N.N. (1987) *Rates and risks for running and exercise injuries: studies in three populations.* Res. Q. Exerc. Sport. 58: 221-228
8 Jacobs, S.J. and Berson, B.L. (1986) *Injuries to runners: a study of entrants to a 10,000-metre race.* Am. J. Sports Med. 14: 151-155
9 Garrick, J.G., Gillian, D.M. and Whiteside, P. (1986) *The epidimeology of aerobic dance injuries.* Am. J. Sports Med. 14: 67-72

Chapter 2

A Complete Rounded Programme

◆ Cross training activities ◆ for general fitness

Many people cross train within a gym or health club environment using treadmills, rowers, steppers and stationery bikes along with resistance machines or free weights, either during the same workout or during separate workouts. The cardio-vascular machines provide training for the heart and lungs (the cardio-respiratory system), and endurance for the muscles, while the fixed resistance or free weights training complement this with increased strength and muscular endurance. By adding flexibility to this, good all-round physical fitness training is accommodated.

Some other common cross training combinations include a choice of walking, swimming, running, rowing, paddling, cycling or aerobic dance to provide cardio-vascular training, adding strength work in the form of weight training or circuit training. Some programmes aim to better accommodate adherence to cardio-vascular training by mixing different cardio-vascular sports, such as running and cycling, running and swimming or, more commonly, all three. As with all forms of training, cross training is far more effective if it is planned.

INTEREST

Reflecting a new approach to fitness for health prevalent in the western world, The English Sports Council published a strategy for sports development in 1997. This strategy laid out a structure containing four areas of development.

1 Foundation – the early development of sporting competence and physical skills upon which all later forms of sports development are based.
2 Participation – sport undertaken primarily for fun, enjoyment, health and fitness and often at basic levels of competence.
3 Performance – a move from participation into a more structured form of competitive sport at county or club level, or at an individual level for personal reasons.
4 Excellence – performance at the highest level of national and international competition.[1]

The first two areas of this development strategy reflect an increasing interest in the training of physical fitness to avoid the onset of disease, improve health and increase quality of life. Where sport and training are intended to meet these needs, cross training ensures a balanced programme and assists long term adherence. Changing the activity offsets boredom and makes the whole session more fun, and choosing complementary activities ensures that all aspects of health related fitness are included in the training.

◆ Flexibility ◆

Some sports, notably martial arts, dancing and gymnastics, which are reliant on high degrees of flexibility for performance, incorporate a lot of flexibility work into their training, thus including these sports as a non-competitive element of a cross training programme may be of benefit. For example, runners may benefit greatly from participating in tai chi, while many bodybuilders benefit from dance training for both the flexibility work and the grace and body awareness needed for posing routines.

Regardless of the activity or sport, every training programme should include flexibility training. Flexibility training ensures that we can move easily and that we are able to twist, turn and reach for all the things we need to, thus enhancing sports performance, improving posture and protecting against injury in everyday life as well as during the playing of sport.

When should I perform my flexibility programme?

Most experts agree that during the warm-up for any exercise or sport it is advisable to put the joints through a full range of movement. It is also agreed that immediately following exercise or sport, as part of the cool-down, one should stretch the muscles that have been worked. In addition, stretching exercises can also be carried out at other times, for example when sitting in front of the fire in the evening, or in small bursts any time during the day.

◆ How do I know what to ◆ include in my cross training programme?

You should primarily choose activities or sports that you enjoy, as this will encourage you to continue training. As your tastes change, change your cross training activities.

Some activities complement each other. For instance, weight training, if done correctly, may enhance rowing performance; cycling may improve or maintain running performance up to a certain distance; and kayaking may add a wet weather sport to the repertoire of someone who participates in a dry weather sport such as rock climbing.

If the sports you enjoy are all heavily reliant on the legs, e.g. cycling and running, you may consider a sport that involves more upper body work such as weight training, swimming or kayaking. If the sports you enjoy are endurance-based, e.g. long distance running or hill walking, you may consider a sport that is more strength/endurance and skill-based such as rock climbing or windsurfing. Finally, if the sports you enjoy are very high intensity, you may consider a lower intensity sport as a complement, for example an ice hockey player may take up walking. Much depends on exactly what you want from your cross training programme.

◆ Cross training and sport ◆

Decathlon, heptathlon and pentathlon have long provided multi-discipline competition, while traditionally, depending on the season, many cyclists and runners at club level and above have competed in road, track and cross country events, each of which provide a slightly different challenge. It was, however, the sudden upsurge of interest in swim, bike and run competitions – the birth of triathlon – that heralded a new era in which multi-discipline sports increased in popularity.

Triathlon

Triathlon is a three-discipline sports competition, normally a combination of swim, bike and run. Two competitive distances have become popular: Olympic distance entailing a 1000m swim, a 40km cycle and a 10km run, and ironman entailing a 2-mile swim, a 72-mile bike ride and a full marathon distance run (26.2 miles).

Other distances are combined to provide sprint triathlons, half ironman and ultra ironman events. Biathlons, involving swim and run, and duathlons, involving a run, bike, run format, are also popular.

Other multi-sport competitions

Triathlons involving other sports are also becoming popular, for example indoor rowing on a rowing **ergometer** such as the Concept II is often combined with a track cycle section and a track run.

DEFINITION

Ergometer – a piece of equipment which is calibrated and produces measurable units of work such that a person's work output can be measured.

For outdoor athletes, kayak, mountain bike and fell run has become a popular competitive combination. Often marketed as a form of triathlon it has paved the way for adventure sports which incorporate events such as running, kayaking, sailing, mountain biking, climbing, riding, cross country skiing, and mountaineering. Challenges such as the Raid Gauloises, the Eco Challenge and the Southern Traverse attract élite athletes with major sponsorship.

Adventure races are usually team events, often requiring the whole team to complete the whole course. Sometimes they are run as a relay and occasionally as single competitor events.

QUOTE

The Countdown Has Begun . . .
Saturday, November 8th, 1997, 9am (NZT)

Geoff and Pascal have begun what must be one of the most hectic weeks anyone could ask for. Last minute preparations, the arrival of international guests and media, a million photocopies, volunteers to organise, and on and on it goes. So too for the competitors who will be anxiously checking equipment, organising their support crews and hoping that these months of hard training are going to be sufficient for what lies ahead. The course is still a highly guarded secret so if you want to find out first I suggest you stay online for the first official release.

This afternoon teams were given a competency test on the ropes rigged up at a local resort in preparation for the new abseiling section of the course. Following this the local college was transformed into briefing H.Q. where the starting point was revealed for the first time. Competitors listened nervously as the long range weather forecast was read out, warning of very cold temperatures and snow and high winds affecting most areas of the course.
EXTRACT FROM A REPORT ON THE SOUTHERN TRAVERSE, 1997 [2]

Indoor cross training challenge competitions such as the Ultrafit competition have increased in popularity with gym and health club members. These involve disciplines drawn from a combination of cardio-vascular machines, callisthenics and resistance equipment.

INTEREST

The UK Ultrafit Challenge

- Indoor cycle 1km
- Indoor row 500m
- Lat pulldown 40 reps (resistance machine)
- Step ups 100 reps
- Press ups 60 reps
- Sit ups 60 reps
- Overhead press 40 reps (resistance machine)
- Treadmill run 800m, 10% incline
- Bench press 40 reps (free weight)

Can cross training be used as training for single sport competition?

The question that many sportspeople ask is: will cross training improve their performance? Scientific research has also considered the question: can you compare the effectiveness of different types of training activities? One study investigated the changes in aerobic capacity in moderately active college-aged students, and discovered similar improvements in **VO₂max** achieved with running and

---

DEFINITION

VO₂max is the highest amount of oxygen that the body can consume for the aerobic production of ATP. That is the amount of oxygen that the body can take in and utilise in the working muscles for the production of energy.

---

with in-line skating programmes provided that the training programmes were equivalent in volume and intensity.[3]

In another study, moderately fit runners trained for four days per week in either run only sessions or alternating run and cycle training at 85–90% maximum heart rate. Both groups significantly improved VO₂max and run performance over 5,000m with no difference between groups.[4]

It would seem from the research available that some transfer of training effects on VO₂max exist from one training mode to another. This, however, seems to be more noticeable when running is performed as a cross training mode, while swim training may result in minimum transfer of training effects on VO₂max.[5] This may, of course, be due to swim training being non-weight bearing and utilising the smaller muscles of the upper body, whereas run training is weight bearing and utilises the large muscles of the legs. If this is the case then one would suppose that activities such as in-line skating would have similar transfer of training effects to that of running so long as both training modes activated similar neural firing patterns and force velocity characteristics. For this reason cross country skiers often use uphill walking as a training activity in preference to running.

DEFINITION

Interval training consists of intermittent exercise with regular rest periods between the work periods. The ratio of work to rest is manipulated according to the desired training effect.

For activities that rely on high levels of maximum oxygen uptake, i.e. endurance-based events, it would therefore seem that appropriate types of cross training, i.e. training that utilises the same muscle groups in the same way, may have a significant effect on VO_2max. However, this training effect never exceeds those induced by sport-specific training, i.e. single discipline training.

Cross training may also lead to a crossover effect between physiological adaptations. For instance, one study showed that during nine weeks of an aerobic **interval training** programme of three-minute work intervals at 90% VO_2max and three-minute rest intervals at 25–40% VO_2max, anaerobic power improved and performance in repeated high-intensity short duration work increased.[6]

The high-intensity aerobic training therefore had a small but nevertheless significant training effect on anaerobic ability – the ability to perform very high-intensity short duration work such as sprinting.

DEFINITION

Anaerobic threshold, also known as onset of blood lactate accumulation (OBLA). The workload at which lactate production is greater than lactate removal and so lactate builds up to such a level that muscular contraction is interfered with.

Improvements in physiology do not always equate to improved performance. Each sport entails a unique combination of demands such as skill, high VO_2max, high **anaerobic threshold** level, high peak power, sustainable power output, psychological ability, etc. It is the combination of these factors that enables the sportsperson to perform at their best. If VO_2max is not the limiting factor for a competitor, then although cross training may help the individual to improve their VO_2max, it may not result in improved performance. A swimmer, for example, may include running in their cross training programme and as a result may improve their VO_2max. However, if it is the muscular endurance of their arms and shoulders that is limiting their performance,

they will not improve as a result of the running element of a cross training programme.

A cyclist may cross train by running or skating to improve VO_2max, but if it is power output on the hills that is limiting their performance, again performance will not improve subsequent to the run training.

The more highly trained an athlete, the more difficult it is to improve performance. For relative beginners, or those less dedicated to training, improvements to any physiological area may improve performance in any one sport.

INTEREST

For the athlete who is dedicated to regular serious training, specificity becomes more of an issue. For these athletes cross training is unlikely to improve performance in a single sport, rather the training must be focused on, and specific to, that sport to allow for the tiny improvements in performance that may mean the difference between winning and losing.

So why should a single sport athlete cross train?

For the single sport athlete cross training may provide some psychological relief and provide a way of maintaining fitness, while reducing the mechanical stresses on the body that are normally associated with high-volume single sport training.

For the injured athlete cross training may provide a way of maintaining fitness while resting the injury and allowing for recovery.

For some athletes cross training can be used when they are unable to participate in their sport, for example ice skaters and hockey players who are restricted to specific ice times. They need to train off the ice as well if they are to get the best from their training programme.

QUOTE

'Cross training is not the key to performing a specific sport at your best. Training in that sport is. In a perfect world, with perfect bodies and no other stresses, we would not need to cross train. So why do it? Because as mere mortals, our bodies get injured, our minds get tired, and our schedules get hectic.

So, cross train to maintain muscular balance and avoid injury. Cross train to correct specific muscular weaknesses. Cross train when time constraints keep you from doing your primary sport, but your body still needs work. Cross train to work your body while resting your mind. In other words, use cross training as a means to an end, always remembering your primary performance goal, and the specific training it requires.'
STEPHEN SEILER, ASSOCIATE PROFESSOR AT THE INSTITUTE OF HEALTH AND SPORT, AGDER COLLEGE, KRISTIANSAND, NORWAY.

INTEREST

- For the general population, cross training may be highly beneficial in terms of overall fitness.
- The principles of specificity of training tend to have greater significance for highly trained athletes.
- Cross training may be an appropriate supplement during rehabilitation periods from physical injury and during periods of overtraining or psychological fatigue.

♦ Do strength and endurance ♦ training successfully combine?

Many endurance athletes in the past have shied away from strength training, believing that excess muscle development will increase their body weight and have a negative impact on their endurance performance. It is well recognised, however, that increases in strength often have a positive effect on endurance performance and are not necessarily accompanied by large increases in muscle bulk.

This was demonstrated in one scientific study in which a combination of heavy resistance training and distance running training improved running economy in serious female recreational runners when compared to a similar group who performed running training alone.[7] Likewise, when studying the strength gains in females who also underwent endurance training it was found there was no impairment of strength development, although the same muscles were used in the endurance training activity.[8]

It does, however, seem evident from the studies done to date that, as with many aspects of training, there is no simple answer to the questions raised regarding the mixing of strength and endurance activities. There is other evidence that high-volume, high-intensity strength training may impair development of high levels of aerobic endurance, and that **muscular hypertrophy** and development of high levels of absolute strength may be inhibited by high-volume, high-intensity aerobic training.

DEFINITION

Muscular hypertrophy is the increase of muscle mass that occurs when the muscle filaments undergo change following resistance work, particularly heavy weight training.

The body is complex and training it is complex. For most people cross training has a positive effect on fitness, however for élite athletes wishing to be competitive at the top end of a single discipline sport, they must be sure of the advantages of cross training before they embark on a cross training programme. For single sport athletes at the top of their sport, cross training will not in itself improve performance, rather training should be specific if it is to increase performance gains. However, if cross training keeps the athlete in the sport and keeps them training, for example by minimising muscle imbalances or injury risk, it may indirectly result in improved performance.

QUOTE
'Combining strength and endurance training is possible without reduced gains in strength or endurance. It is probably frequency of training that is the most important factor in combined training.'[9]   McCarthy

◆ What are the advantages ◆ and disadvantages of cross training?

Advantages	Disadvantages
Cross training is an appropriate form of training for all-round fitness for most individuals.	
Multi-sport participants need to cross train in the disciplines most relevant to their sport.	High-volume, high-intensity aerobic training may inhibit development of high levels of absolute strength or muscular hypertrophy.
Single sport competitors may benefit from cross training in the form of injury prevention and rehabilitation.	For single sport competitors specific training will yield higher levels of sports performance for élite athletes.
Strength and endurance training are mutually compatible and mutually beneficial for most people.	High-volume, high-intensity strength training may inhibit development of high levels of aerobic endurance.

1 *England the Sporting Nation: a strategy for sport in England.* The English Sports Council (1997)

2 Taken from the Southern Traverse website – http\www.southern traverse.com

3 Melanson, E.L., Freedson, P.S. and Jungbluth, S. (1996) *Changes in VO_2max and maximal treadmill time after nine weeks of running or in line skate training.* Med. Sci. Sport and Exerc. 28 (11) 1422–6

4 Mutton, D.L., Loy, S.F., Rogers, D.M., Holland, J.G., Vincent, W.J. and Heng, M. (1993) *Effect of run vs combined cycle/run training on VO_2max and running performance.* Med. Sci. Sport and Exerc. 25 (12) 1393–7

5 Tanaka, H. (1994) *Effects of cross training. Transfer of training effects on VO_2max between cycling, running and swimming.* Sports Med. 18: 5, 330–9

6 Gaiga, M.C. and Docherty, D. (1995) *The effect of an aerobic interval training programme on intermittent anaerobic performance.* Can. J. Appl. Physiol. 20 (4): 452–64

7 Johnston, R.E., Quinn, T.J., Kertzer, R. and Vroman, N.B. (1995) *Strength training on female distance runners: impact on running economy.* Med. Sci. Sport and Exerc. 27 (5) supplement

8 Blessing, D.L., Gravelle, B.L., Wang, Y.T. and Kim, K.C. (1995) *The influence of co-activation on the adaptive response to concurrent strength and endurance training in women.* Med. Sci. Sport and Exerc. 27 (5) supplement

9 McCarthy et al. (1995) *Compatibility of adaptive responses with combining strength and endurance training.* Med. Sci. Sport and Exerc. 27 (3) 429–36

How Does it All Work?

Chapter 3

Muscle

The body is a very smart machine, each part integrating and working in unison with the other parts. As with man-made machines, if the body is not well maintained it will begin to disintegrate. However, unlike man-made machines, this machine has the ability to adapt to unaccustomed stress. Training is simply a way of imposing that unaccustomed stress to persuade the body to adapt.

The physiological adaptations that occur are dependent on the type of unaccustomed stress that is applied. They occur to allow the body to cope more easily with the physical demands placed upon it. Thus, if we lift a heavy object regularly we become more able to lift heavy objects, i.e. we become stronger. If we spend a lot of time walking we adapt and are able to walk further or faster and with less effort.

To understand how to train effectively we must understand something of the physiology of the body and of how it adapts to different exercise demands.

To understand how to cross train effectively we must have some understanding of the interaction of different training methods and the effect they have on performance.

When we train we effect changes in muscle, in metabolism, in the nervous system, in the bones and connective tissues, and in the mind.

◆ Muscle ◆

There are three types of muscle found in the body: **cardiac muscle**, **smooth muscle** and **striated muscle**.

DEFINITION

Cardiac muscle is the muscle found in the heart.
Smooth muscle is found in the gastrointestinal tract.
Striated or **skeletal muscle** is the muscle which is attached to the skeletal system and is under voluntary control.

Striated muscle is the muscle that we use to maintain posture and effect movement. This is also the muscle that is of importance in relation to fitness, specifically in relation to **muscular strength**, **muscular endurance** and **power**.

There is sometimes confusion in the area of muscular fitness in that strength and endurance are often treated as completely separate issues. The term 'strength' is often used to include both muscular strength and muscular endurance, whereas the term 'endurance' is often thought of purely as a cardio-vascular issue. In reality, strength and endurance are each a function of both muscle fitness and metabolic fitness.

DEFINITION

- **Force** is something that causes an object to be formed or moved.
- **Muscular strength** is an expression of the amount of force generated by one single maximum contraction. It refers to the ability of a muscle or group of muscles to exert maximum force to overcome a resistance.
- **Muscular endurance** is the ability of a muscle or group of muscles to exert force to overcome a resistance for an extended period of time. It is an expression of the ability to repeatedly generate muscular force.
- **Power** is the product of force and velocity, or strength x speed. Power = (force x distance)/time.

How do muscles contract?

To understand this it is helpful to understand something of the structure of muscle. If we take a single muscle fibre or muscle cell and examine it we find that it is made up of myo-filaments. These are tiny filaments of proteins called actin and myosin. When a muscle fibre is innervated to contract, these actin and myosin filaments (myofilaments) slide across each other causing the muscle to contract. This is known as the sliding filament theory.

Imagine that you have bought some coloured pencils as a gift. You buy the pencils and then think of a way to wrap them to make the parcel more exciting. Let's say that you wrap each single pencil in red paper and you leave paper sticking out at the ends of the pencils like a Christmas cracker. Then

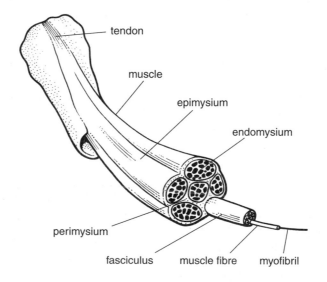

Figure 3.1 The anatomy of muscle

you arrange the pencils into little bundles, and wrap each in green paper, again leaving the green paper sticking out at the ends. Next, bundle all the little green packages together and wrap the whole lot in blue paper, again leaving the blue paper sticking out at the ends.

This is similar to the structure of muscle. The pencils are the single muscle fibres, each individually wrapped in connective tissue, endomysium, which extends beyond the fibres (as the red paper wraps the pencils). The fibres are bundled together to form fasciculi, each of which is wrapped in connective tissue, perimysium, which extends beyond the fibres (as the green paper wraps the pencil bundles). The fasciculi are then bundled together to form the complete muscle which is wrapped in connective tissue, epimysium, which extends beyond the fibres (as the blue paper wraps the whole present).

Thus there is connective tissue running throughout the muscle and extending beyond the muscle fibres where it forms the strong **tendons** which attach muscle to bone.

How does this cause movement?

The actin and myosin filaments are the contractile part of the muscle fibre, and the connective tissue extends from the ends of the muscle to form the strong connective tissue of the tendons which are attached into the **periosteum** or outer wrapping of the bones.

> ### DEFINITION
> **Tendons** are the connective tissues that attach muscle to bone.
> **Periosteum** is the connective tissue sheath wrapped around bone.

Each muscle is attached across a joint – one end is attached to one bone of a joint and the other end is attached to the other bone – thus when the muscle contracts the force generated is transmitted through the tendons and pulls on the bones to which the tendons are attached. As the muscles pull on the bones across a joint they cause movement to occur at that joint.

Muscles can only pull

The muscles can only pull, they cannot push, thus to return a joint to its original position, and a muscle to its resting length, a second force must operate. This may be an external force such as gravity, or it may be force from a contraction in the opposing muscle group.

For example, if the biceps muscle group contracts to flex the arm at the elbow joint, the elbow may return to its resting position simply because of the force of gravity or because the triceps muscle group is contracting, as when we extend the elbow in a pushing movement.

What causes the muscle to contract?

A muscle is stimulated to contract by the nerves feeding it. The nerve centres in the brain relay messages down the spinal column and out through the **efferent nerve** pathways to the muscle fibres.

> ### DEFINITION
> **Efferent nerves** are motor nerves. They transmit messages from the central nervous system to the rest of the body.

Each nerve ending serves a number of muscle fibres. The nerve ending and its associated muscle fibres are known collectively as a motor unit. When a motor nerve stimulates a contraction, all of the fibres in that motor unit must contract fully. This is known as the 'all or nothing' principle.

Therefore, if only a small amount of force is required the stimulus for the fibres to contract is relayed down only a few nerve pathways and so only a few muscle fibres in that muscle will contract, thus generating a low contractile force.

FACT

The force generated by muscular contraction is dependent on the number of motor units firing, thus to lift a pencil the body needs only to recruit a few motor units as the force of contraction needed is small, while to lift a heavy weight the body needs to recruit a large number of motor units.

Likewise, to run slowly requires a lower force of contraction than to run fast, and therefore the recruitment of fewer motor units.

If, on the other hand, a large contractile force is required, the stimulus to contract is relayed down a large number of nerve fibres resulting in a large number of fibres contracting and generating a high force.

Where the body needs relatively small amounts of force but very fine control, as in the fingers for example, each motor unit contains only a small number of muscle fibres or contractile units. Where the body generally needs to generate much higher forces but with less fine control, such as in the legs, each motor unit contains a large number of contractile units.

FACT

The activation and control of voluntary muscles works on an 'all or nothing' principle. Within each muscle, muscle fibres are grouped into units controlled by motor nerves. Each group of muscle fibres and the nerve that stimulates them to contract is known as a motor unit. When the nerve feeding a single motor unit fires, all the muscle fibres within that motor unit must contract fully. The strength of the muscular contraction is dependent on how many motor units fire. This is known as the 'all or nothing' principle.

What causes the actin and myosin filaments to slide across each other?

The interface between the nerve ending and the muscle cell is known as the motor end plate. The nerve fibre transmits an electrical stimulus which causes the chemical acetylcholine to be released at the motor end plate. This chemical causes a change in the permeability of the muscle membrane to sodium and potassium ions, and triggers an electrical charge to be transmitted the full length of the muscle fibre and through the muscle fibre in a network of tubules to the interior of the muscle cell. This causes an increase in free calcium ions in the muscle cell which in turn causes the actin and myosin filaments to slide across each other.

The acetylcholine released from the motor end plate is almost immediately destroyed by the enzyme cholinesterase and the calcium ions begin to move away from the actin and myosin filaments. This is associated with the relaxation of the muscle fibre. Once it is relaxed another force such as gravity or the contraction of an opposing muscle can move the joint in the opposite direction, lengthening the muscle cell once again and returning the actin and myosin filaments to their resting position.

Types of muscular contractions

Isometric

In an isometric contraction force is created but no movement across the joint occurs. Holding on to an object, e.g. carrying a suitcase, employs this type of contraction; the contraction serves to fix the joint or group of joints into position. When we are upright we employ many isometric contractions to overcome the force of gravity and hold us in an upright position, thus isometric contractions are central to maintaining posture.

Isotonic

An isotonic contraction is one in which there is movement around a joint. Most free movement involves isotonic contractions at some joints and isometric contractions to stabilise others. For example, flexing the fingers employs isotonic contractions in the front of the forearm to move the fingers, and isometric contractions in the back of the forearm to fix the wrist in position and prevent it from flexing as well.

Isokinetic

An isokinetic contraction is one in which the speed of movement around a joint is controlled by an external force. Some exercise machines are engineered to control the speed of movement, such that however much force is generated by the muscle the speed of limb movement remains constant throughout the contraction.

The two phases of a muscular contraction involving movement can be further classified as concentric and eccentric.

Concentric

During a concentric contraction the two ends of a muscle move closer together and the muscle length shortens. Lifting the arm above the head involves a concentric contraction of the deltoid muscle; flexing the arm at the elbow joint involves a concentric contraction of the biceps muscle.

Eccentric

When a muscle is generating force in an attempt to overcome a resistance but is in fact lengthening (giving in to the resistance), it is working in the eccentric phase of the contraction. This occurs, for instance, when lowering an object to the floor under control, or when lowering oneself into a chair.

Strength training is an important part of injury prevention and of post injury rehabilitation. An increase in the strength of a muscle, or group of muscles, will afford protection for the joint(s) across which the strengthened muscles run. Thus strength work for the quadriceps and hamstrings is important in the rehabilitation of knee injuries, and abdominal work (as well as back strengthening exercises) is important in the rehabilitation of back injuries. The abdominal muscles cross the anterior side of the spinal column due to the fact that they run vertically down the front of the torso. They are used to help 'fix' the spine in a safe position during activities.

If a muscle or group of muscles is extremely weak, such as after prolonged bed rest, then any activity, even if normally classified as an endurance activity, is likely to increase the strength capabilities of that group of muscles.

Likewise, as each motor unit becomes stronger, following heavy resistance training for example, then fewer motor units are needed to complete a given maximum workload, thus creating a greater motor unit reserve and increasing endurance capabilities.

The first response of a muscle to strength or resistance training involves neurogenic changes; the nerves controlling the firing pattern of the muscle become more efficient, so increasing the strength in any given movement without any changes to the muscle itself. Thus from an untrained state huge increases in muscular strength may be made without any increase in muscle mass at all.

Secondly, changes are made within the muscle itself. These are known as myogenic changes and involve an increase in the density or the size of the muscle.

Two theories explain the way in which a muscle increases in size. The theory of hypertrophy and the theory of hyperplasia. At the present time there is little evidence of hyperplasia in human muscle, thus scientific support for the theory of hypertrophy is greater than that for the theory of hyperplasia, though it should be noted that support for one theory does not necessarily rule out the other.

So do myogenic changes always result in an increase in size?

The answer to this question rather depends on what is meant by size. Let's assume hypertrophy occurs during your strength training programme, i.e. there is an increase in the number of the myofilaments within each muscle cell.

Hypertrophy

Imagine a tube of Smarties in which some of the Smarties have been eaten so the tube is half empty. The tube remains the same size, but it will easily squash. Now imagine the tube is packed full – it becomes a very firm, non-squashy, nicely toned tube of Smarties. It is still the same size as before, but is now 'toned'. If, however, the tube had elastic walls, you could keep on stuffing Smarties into it until the walls bulged and the dimensions of the tube had increased.

Likewise, increasing the myofilaments within a muscle will at first tone the muscle. The difference is that you *can* continue stuffing new myofilaments into your muscle cells until the whole muscle increases in size.

Of course, when you start strength training the first changes that will happen are neurogenic changes: no increase in size, just improvements in strength. If you continue to progress your training you will eventually start to get myogenic changes: an increase in the number of myofilaments, the first effect of which will be to tone up the muscle.

No progression in training equals no increase in size

The body is very clever and doesn't like to be wasteful. If you are coping well with your training it will not bother to make any adaptations – it doesn't need to. Thus if you have increased the number of myofilaments until you are looking toned but don't increase your training level at all, you will simply stay toned and will not increase in size. Similarly, changing your type of resistance training may continue to improve power, strength or endurance without any further increase in muscle size. Further, it has been shown that increases in muscle mass are most often accompanied by a reduction in body fat, so despite the fact that muscle mass may increase, total size may not, and may even be reduced.

Whatever your resistance training routine, be assured that building large amounts of muscle mass, as seen in competitive bodybuilding, requires very high-volume, high-intensity resistance work, even for those people who have the genetic ability to make large increases in muscle size.

For women, building muscle mass is even more difficult as they simply do not have the correct hormones to build size easily. Those few women who are successful in building muscle mass work extremely hard with heavy resistance training. For most of us this type of success is just not possible.

I need good flexibility so I do not want to become 'muscle bound'

There is no evidence that strength training impairs flexibility[1]. On the contrary, gymnasts, rock climbers and dancers are extremely flexible and also extremely strong. It takes great strength to lift a straight leg so that your toes are at shoulder height, and hold it there; it takes great strength to hold on to a tiny crack in a rock and pull your whole body weight up on one hand; and it takes great strength to hold your body in a crucifix on the rings.

Olympic weightlifters performing a clean and jerk or a snatch show an excellent range of motion in the ankles, knees, hips and shoulders, without which they would not be capable of performing the lifts. Bodybuilders, despite their size, are also often capable of demonstrating remarkable flexibility during their posing routines, many being capable of achieving the splits.

It is not strength training that reduces a person's range of motion, but rather it is not using that range of motion regularly that is inhibitory.

OPINION

- Increases in strength can be very beneficial to all sportspersons in stabilising and maintaining joint integrity; in reducing the percentage of effort needed to complete a task; and in withstanding the forces on the body during sports performance.
- Increases in strength are not necessarily accompanied by large increases in body mass or a reduction in flexibility.
- For sports performance strength training should be specific. Gymnasts, for example, need a good power–weight ratio and also need strength training specific to those joints that are at risk because of the high degrees of flexibility demanded during their performance.

1 Barton, L., Bird, H.A., Lindsay, M., Newton, J. and Wright, V. (1995) *The effect of different joint interventions on the range of movement at a joint.* Journal of Orthopaedic Rheumatology (United Kingdom) 8/2, 87–92

Chapter 4

Metabolism

◆ Metabolism ◆

The body's response to exercise is in part dependent upon its ability to store and utilise the fuels which provide the power for muscular contraction. The higher the intensity of the activity the quicker energy must be supplied for muscular contraction. If we train the body to use fuels efficiently then we fatigue less quickly.

In order to train the body to use fuels efficiently we must first understand something about the use of those fuels.

We eat foodstuffs containing fats and carbohydrates to supply us with energy. These are broken down and stored in the body until energy is needed. However, whichever fuel we use to provide energy, that energy can only be used for muscular contraction if it is first converted into the chemical adenosine tri-phosphate (ATP). Thus the stored fats and carbohydrates must be processed so that their energy store can be converted into ATP before it is used to fuel muscular contraction. The energy is simply converted from one format to another.

FACT

Energy can neither be created nor destroyed, only converted.

◆ Energy from the sun ◆

In a similar way we use the energy from the sun. Energy is released as heat and light from the sun and is used by plants for growth. The plants trap the energy from light and, through a process called photosynthesis, use that energy to grow.

Some of them become huge trees, which when they die are buried in the ground and become coal. We dig the coal out of the ground and burn it to provide heat, some of which we may use to boil water. The water gives off steam which we use to drive turbines, which provide electricity which we use to power our homes, providing heat, light and the power to drive the vacuum cleaner, the television, the microwave oven, etc. Thus energy is released from the sun, trapped in different ways and converted into forms that we can use.

◆ How does ATP work? ◆

Adenosine tri-phosphate is made up of one molecule of adenosine and three phosphate molecules, attached by high energy bonds. Energy is trapped inside these bonds. When ATP is broken down one of the high energy bonds is broken and energy is released. This energy is used to fuel muscular contraction. When the high energy bond is broken ATP is

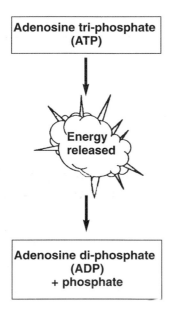

Adenosine tri-phosphate (ATP)

↓

Energy released

↓

Adenosine di-phosphate (ADP) + phosphate

Figure 4.1 ATP is broken down to form adenosine di-phosphate and one free phosphate molecule

split forming adenosine di-phosphate (ADP) and one free phosphate molecule.

This process is reversible. If energy is added to ADP and a free phosphate molecule, ATP is formed. Thus by adding energy from other sources we can replenish our ATP stores.

Energy released from splitting ATP is the only energy that can be utilised for muscular contraction. Our muscles have a limited store of ATP which, as it is used up, must be replenished from other sources. The energy systems known as the aerobic and anaerobic systems break down fats and carbohydrates and a substance called creatine-phosphate which then release their stores of energy. This energy is used to replenish the stores of ATP. The amount of ATP in the cells must remain constant if we are to avoid an energy crisis. The ATP therefore needs to be constantly recycled.

Adenosine di-phosphate (ADP) + phosphate

↓

Energy

↓

Adenosine tri-phosphate (ATP)

Figure 4.2 The process outlined in figure 4.1 is reversed and ATP is created

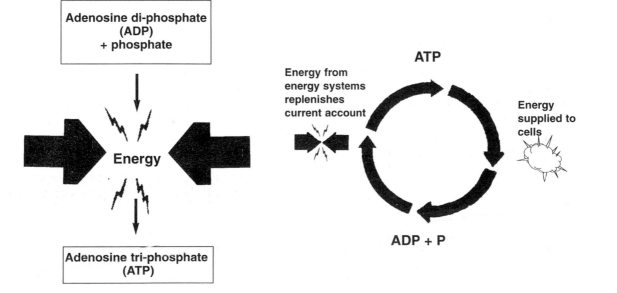

Energy from energy systems replenishes current account

ATP

Energy supplied to cells

ADP + P

Figure 4.3 The cyclic nature of the ATP/ADP system

♦ Short term energy supplies ♦ – the anaerobic systems

The creatine-phosphate system and the lactic acid system, also known as anaerobic glycolysis, are anaerobic in nature, that is they do not need oxygen in order to release energy.

The creatine-phosphate system

When the muscles are at rest ATP is recycled at a steady rate, supplying the small amount of energy that is needed. When we suddenly require significantly more energy, as is the case when we start to move around, then more ATP is split to release energy more rapidly. When this happens, unless the delivery of energy from the energy systems is speeded up significantly, the muscles' store of ATP would be emptied very quickly.

Creatine-phosphate, which is stored in the muscles, can be broken down to release energy.

INTEREST

Stored creatine-phosphate can supply enough energy to:

- walk briskly for one minute
- run for 20–30 seconds
- perform an all-out sprint for around six seconds.[1]

Creatine-phosphate is very responsive to the needs of the muscles and is capable of supplying energy very quickly but only for an extremely short period of time. This system is sometimes thought of as the start-up system. Like a car battery which supplies a sudden burst of energy to start the car, this system can supply a sudden burst of energy to start the muscles moving.

The creatine-phosphate system is also utilised during very high-intensity activity when the demand for the fast delivery of energy is such that the other energy systems cannot meet it, for example during short sprints, or when lifting an extremely heavy weight.

Also, like the energy from a car battery, the energy from the creatine-phosphate system is drained very quickly. By running a car at a steady pace for a while energy from the fuel system can be utilised to recharge the car battery; similarly, energy from the aerobic system is utilised to recreate creatine-phosphate and replenish this system.

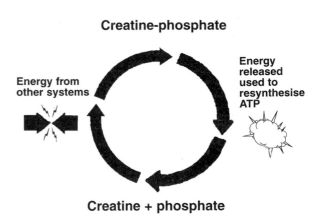

Creatine-phosphate

Energy from other systems

Energy released used to resynthesise ATP

Creatine + phosphate

Figure 4.4 The cyclic nature of the creatine-phosphate system

Lactic acid system or anaerobic glycolysis

The other anaerobic system is anaerobic glycolysis. This system utilises carbohydrate which is stored in the body as glycogen, converting it into glucose and then into a

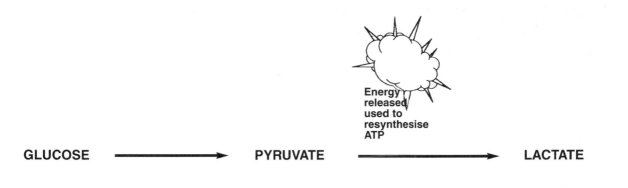

Figure 4.5 *Anaerobic glycolysis*

substance called pyruvate. Pyruvate is broken down further to release energy.

This system also supplies energy (to replenish ATP) at a high rate, however in doing so it releases lactate which builds up in the form of lactic acid. Lactic acid build-up in the muscle blocks muscle contraction causing a burning sensation and pain, forcing the body to slow down or stop when the intensity of exercise is too high for too long a period of time. Thus lactic acid build-up is a safety mechanism. It takes between 45 seconds and three minutes of very high-intensity exercise for the lactate to build up enough to block muscular contraction.

High-intensity exercise

Creatine-phosphate and anaerobic glycolysis systems support high-intensity exercise and also provide a reservoir of energy for sudden bursts of movement. However, these systems are short term. When energy supplies must be maintained during long duration exercise, the anaerobic systems are supplementary to the breakdown of carbohydrate and fat by the aerobic system.

◆ Long term energy supplies ◆ – the aerobic system

The aerobic system oxidises fat or carbohydrate, releasing energy (to replenish ATP), and leaving carbon dioxide and water as by-products.

Fat/carbohydrate + Oxygen → Carbon dioxide + Water

The carbon dioxide is transported to the lungs and expelled, while the water is utilised within the body.

This process provides most of our energy requirements throughout the day. At low to moderate levels of intensity of exercise, the body can continue to recycle ATP for hours, largely from these aerobic sources.

Aerobic respiration is only possible within organelles called **mitochondria**, found within the muscle cell.

DEFINITION

Mitochondria are the sites within the muscle cell where aerobic metabolism – the oxidation of fats and carbohydrates – takes place.

The use of fat as fuel

The body stores large amounts of energy as fat. Fat is a very rich energy store; 1g of fat stores 9kcals whereas 1g of carbohydrate stores only 4kcals. However, the breakdown of fat to release energy utilises large amounts of oxygen. The body's limited ability to supply large amounts of oxygen to the muscles limits the intensity of exercise that can be fuelled by fat, thus the anaerobic systems which supply energy at a very high rate but do not use oxygen cannot utilise fat as fuel. High-intensity exercise is mainly fuelled by carbohydrate and creatine-phosphate. Low-intensity, long duration exercise relies much more on fat as a fuel.

Oxidisation

$$FAT + O_2 \longrightarrow CO_2 + H_2O$$

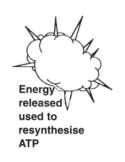

Energy released used to resynthesise ATP

Figure 4.6 The use of fat as fuel

The use of carbohydrate as fuel

Carbohydrate in the form of glucose can also be used as fuel by the aerobic system.

Whatever the form of carbohydrate we take into our body as food, it is always broken down into glucose. Carbohydrate is stored in the form of glycogen in the liver and in skele-

tal muscle, and this is then reconverted into glucose before it is further broken down in the presence of oxygen to release energy. The complete breakdown or oxidisation of glucose to carbon dioxide and water releases energy which is used to resynthesise ATP.

Oxidisation

$$GLUCOSE + O_2 \longrightarrow CO_2 + H_2O$$

Energy released used to resynthesise ATP

Figure 4.7 The use of carbohydrate as fuel

This is very much a simplification of the process. In reality the breakdown of glucose is a two-tiered system.

The glucose is first converted to pyruvate and the pyruvate is transported into the mitochondria of the muscle where, in the presence of oxygen, it is broken down to form carbon dioxide and water, releasing energy.

Therefore the rate of this process is limited by how quickly the pyruvate can be transported into the mitochondria. If the glucose is broken down into pyruvate faster than it can be transported into the mitochondria, the backlog of pyruvate is dispersed by turning it into lactate. This process is anaerobic glycolysis (*see* page 30).

The accumulating lactate may be cleared from the muscle cell into the bloodstream, or it may be reconverted into pyruvate and transported into the mitochondria, to be utilised in the aerobic system.

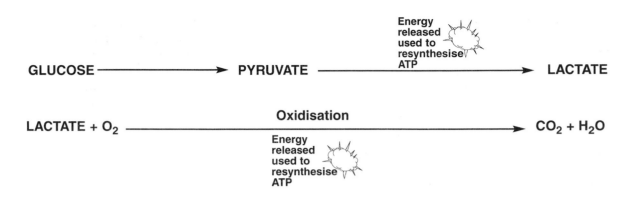

Figure 4.8 Two-tier system

The possible fates of pyruvate:

1 Pyruvate enters the Krebbs cycle in mitochondria. Pyruvate $+ O_2 \to CO_2 + H_2O$. This process releases enough energy for 36 molecules of ATP.

2 When the rate of pyruvate production exceeds the rate of entry into mitochondria the pyruvate is converted into lactate. This process releases enough energy for two molecules of ATP.

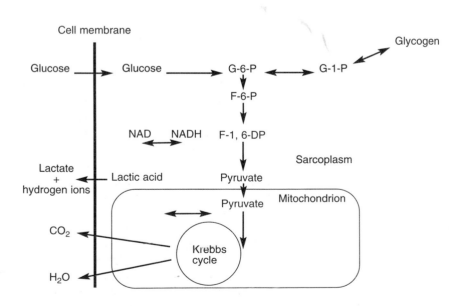

Figure 4.9 Metabolic pathways

♦ The utilisation of fuels ♦

As we start exercising there is a delay in achieving steady state aerobic metabolism when oxygen consumption and supply are equal. Thus the energy used at the beginning of exercise is largely supplied by the anaerobic systems, creatine-phosphate and anaerobic glycolysis. As time progresses there is an increasing contribution from the aerobic system until nearly all the cost of the exercise is met by aerobic metabolism. This is known as 'steady state'.

INTEREST

There is an oxygen deficit at the start of exercise, at which time energy is supplied by the anaerobic systems. As oxygen supply is ramped up to meet the increased demand, there is an increasing contribution from the aerobic system until nearly all the cost of the exercise is met by aerobic metabolism.

If the intensity of the exercise increases such that the rate at which energy is needed is so great that the aerobic system can no longer supply energy fast enough to cope with the demand, the contribution from anaerobic sources must once more increase. Thus the rate of conversion of pyruvate to lactate increases and lactate starts to build up in the muscle cells.

FACT

The body will clear this lactate from the muscles as fast as it is able to by:

- transporting the lactate into the bloodstream
- shunting the lactate to nearby muscle cells
- continuing to increase the supply of oxygen and transport of pyruvate into the mitochondria and converting the lactate back to pyruvate.

If we are unable to increase aerobic metabolism enough to keep clearing the lactate however, it will continue to build up until eventually we reach a threshold where the build-up starts to interfere with muscular contraction. This intensity is variously known as anaerobic threshold, aerobic threshold or onset of blood lactate accumulation (OBLA).

If, despite the increase in the intensity of exercise, we are able to remain below threshold level, then we will gradually reach steady state again. Regular training allows a person to reach steady state sooner, i.e. there is less oxygen deficit.

What happens to the lactate in the bloodstream?

- Lactic acid in the muscle disassociates to form lactate and hydrogen ions which enter the bloodstream independently. Sodium bicarbonate in the blood buffers the hydrogen ions by forming sodium lactate and the weak carbonic acid.

Lactic acid in muscle →
Lactate and Hydrogen ions in blood

- Lactate in the bloodstream is transported to the liver where it is reconverted into glycogen.
- The carbonic acid (H_2CO_3) changes the pH of the blood but is relatively unstable. It will readily disassociate to produce carbon dioxide and water. The increased carbon dioxide causes a rise in the rate of ventilation, that is respiratory compensation for the metabolic acidosis.

> Sodium bicarbonate + Lactate + Hydrogen ions → Sodium lactate + Carbonic acid (H_2CO_3)
>
> Carbonic acid (H_2CO_3)→
> Water H_2O + Carbon dioxide CO_2

- Physically this is evident by heavy breathing after the exercise has stopped. The sportsperson is paying back the oxygen debt.
- It is well documented that individuals who participate in high-intensity training are more able to tolerate high lactic acid concentrations and acid blood pH. Whether this is as a result of increased ability to buffer the acid in the blood or whether it is a result of a greater psychological threshold is unclear.

---

1 McArdle, Katch and Katch. *Exercise Physiology* (3rd edition). Lea and Febiger. p. 123

Chapter 5

Fibre Types

Scientific research has shown that not all muscle fibres are the same. They differ in contractile speed, in enzyme characteristics and in **metabolic enzyme profile**. Thus muscle is classified into different fibre types.

DEFINITION

Metabolic enzyme profile – muscle fibres can be identified by distinguishing the enzymes characteristic of the different energy systems that they use.

Muscle fibres are categorised as slow twitch or fast twitch fibres based on the time it takes for them to reach peak tension once they are stimulated to contract. Slow twitch fibres are also called type I fibres, while fast twitch fibres are called type II fibres.

Muscle fibres can also be classified based on their metabolic properties, thus type I fibres may be termed slow oxidative fibres. They have a lot of mitochondria and oxidative enzymes, a plentiful supply of capillaries and are well adapted for aerobic respiration. Type II fibres may be termed fast glycolytic fibres. They are well adapted for anaerobic respiration, and reach peak tension very quickly.

Are there more than two fibre types?

Based on metabolic properties, type II or fast twitch muscle fibres can be further divided into sub-categories. At least two types of fast twitch fibre have been identified: type IIB fibres, also called fast glycolytic (FG), and type IIA fibres, also called fast oxidative glycolytic (FOG). The FG fibres store **glycogen** and have high levels of the enzymes necessary for producing energy anaerobically, but they contain relatively few mitochondria. The FOG fibres are similar to the FG fibres, but are capable of adapting and increasing their ability to utilise oxygen, by increasing their number of mitochondria, **oxidative enzymes** and blood capillaries. These adaptations occur with training and result in a person being able to work at higher intensities while utilising aerobic respiration, in other words greater endurance at higher intensities.

DEFINITION

Glycogen is the body's store of carbohydrate.
Oxidative enzymes are the enzymes involved in aerobic metabolism.

Slow twitch fibres are fatigue resistant and so are associated with endurance events.

Type I – slow oxidative (SO)	Type IIA – fast oxidative glycolytic (FOG)	Type IIB – fast glycolytic (FG)
• Plentiful supply of capillaries. • Lots of mitochondria. • Lots of oxidative enzymes. • Well adapted to aerobic respiration. • Reach peak tension more slowly. • Slow to start. • Fatigue resistant.	• Similar to FG fibres but with training are capable of adapting to aerobic respiration.	• Poorer supply of capillaries. • Fewer mitochondria. • Lots of anaerobic enzymes. • Well adapted to anaerobic respiration. • Reach peak tension quickly. • Quick to start. • Quick to fatigue.

Fast glycolytic fibres reach peak tension very quickly and so are associated with sprint and power events, such as throwing and jumping events, and Olympic weight lifting. In these events an abundance of fast glycolytic fibres is important as peak force must be produced very quickly.

How many fast twitch and slow twitch fibres do I have?

Within the body, muscles have different fibre compositions. The long head of the triceps at the back of the arm, for example, is predominantly made up of fast twitch fibres, while the vastus lateralis found in the front of the thigh has a very mixed fibre-type profile, and the gluteal muscles of the buttocks are primarily slow twitch dominated. Some muscles in the body are very endurance-based, for instance the main function of the muscles of the trunk and lower back, the abdominal muscles, is postural. They need not apply force quickly, however they do need to apply enough force to hold us upright and maintain our posture for long periods of time. These muscles therefore have a greater number of slow twitch than fast twitch fibres.

INTEREST

At the age of 47, British marathon runner Leslie Watson competed at national level in the 1997 British Powerlifting Championships. She had successfully changed from being a national level endurance sport champion to being a national level strength sport champion.

It is well known that marathon runners possess a high percentage of slow twitch fibres, so why was Leslie Watson able to change her training and become a national level powerlifter?

Each of the fibre types produce the same amount of force. It is the rate at which they can reach peak tension, the rate of force production, that is different.

In relatively short, high-intensity events where the rate of achieving peak tension is not an issue, such as powerlifting or truck pulling, the peak force generated rather than the speed at which it is generated is important. Thus these athletes may have more slow oxidative fibres – type is not an issue.

In muscles with a heterogeneous mix of fibre types the majority of people have a reasonably even number of fast twitch and slow twitch fibres, however some people have a greater number of fast twitch fibres and these people will be better adapted for power events. Other people have a greater number of slow twitch fibres and are thus better adapted for endurance.

If I am an endurance athlete do I only use slow twitch fibres?

No. Endurance events also require power to produce speed, but rather than short bursts of power these events require sustained power such that a world class male marathon runner can run at just under five-minute mile pace for over two hours.

INTEREST

Endurance events require sustained power. World class male marathon runners run at just under five-minute mile pace for over two hours, while world class heavy weight male rowers (2,000m) produce power outputs of around 460 watts for just under six minutes.

For endurance sports then, training the fast twitch type IIA fibres to utilise oxygen and accumulate less lactate is of prime importance in increasing sustained power output.

How do I know which fibre types I am using?

The fibre types activated depends on the force of contraction needed. At low intensities type I fibres (slow oxidative) are recruited. At higher intensities type IIA (fast oxidative glycolytic fibres) are also recruited, and at extremely high intensities both these fibre types and the type IIB (fast glycolytic) fibres are recruited. There is a gradual ramping up of fibre type recruitment as the intensity of the exercise increases.

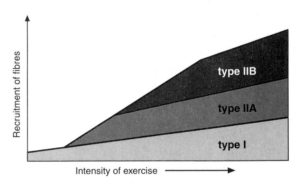

Figure 5.1 Fibre type recruitment

♦ Strength ♦

Absolute strength requires high total force production irrespective of the rate of force production, and is a result of the number of fibre types, both slow and fast, that are recruited and the size of the muscle.

The strength of a muscle is directly proportional to cross sectional area of the muscle. A weak elephant will therefore still be stronger than a strong horse simply because its muscles are bigger. For this reason, in strength sports such as powerlifting it would be unfair for a large person to compete against a small person, thus strength related sports are characterised by weight classes.

Do I use fast twitch or slow twitch fibres when I train for strength?

In order to perform one maximal lift as in powerlifting, all the available muscle fibres must be recruited, both slow and fast twitch. The type IIB fibres will fatigue during that one maximal effort so that lift will not be achieved again until recovery of those fibres is complete. However, the powerlifter would immediately be able to lift a lighter weight which recruited type I fibres and, with this lighter weight, would very probably achieve more than one repetition.

Increases in strength are partially due to neurogenic changes, that is changes in the nervous system, and partially due to changes in the contractile elements of the muscle, the myofilaments. Initially improvements in strength come from learning to recruit more fibres to achieve the task, or, more accurately, learning to recruit as many fibres as possible in the right sequence to achieve the task with greater efficiency and force production. Further increases in strength occur at a myogenic level. The myofilaments actin and myosin increase in size and number thus increasing their contractile force.

To get stronger, do I need to get bigger?

Many athletes are concerned that if they put on weight they will have more weight to carry around and will therefore become slower, so they shy away from strength training. In reality great strength gains can be made without any increase in weight at all. By working at very specific strength training, increases in strength due to neurogenic changes may benefit the athlete. For instance a shot putter may use a heavier shot in training than in competition; a swimmer may use hand paddles to increase the resistance afforded by the water; and a cross country skier may spend a lot of time double poling up hill to increase upper body strength. Further strength gains may be due to changes in the size of the muscle, however this is not necessarily counterproductive.

Increases in muscle mass, especially in older athletes, are often accompanied by a reduction in fat mass.[1] As muscle is metabolically active, an increase in mass has the effect of increasing the metabolic rate and helping to maintain low body fat levels.[2] Often athletes starting a strength training programme notice that when they stand on the scales their weight hasn't changed despite the improved muscle tone. The increase in muscle has been accompanied by a reduction in body fat, so overall weight hasn't changed. Further, while fat is in effect dead weight for the athlete to carry around, muscle produces force. Often a slight increase in weight is offset by the much greater increase in power.

Finally, athletic activity produces large forces in the joints. It is the musculature around the joint that counteracts these forces, stabilising it and holding it together during sport. Many injuries occur and reoccur because the **fixator muscles** around the joint are not strong enough to do this job, therefore strengthening these muscles may prevent injury, allowing the athlete to train more consistently and so improve performance.

> **DEFINITION**
>
> **Fixator muscles** check unwanted movement in a joint or joint complex.

Strength training and health

Many of our everyday activities involve strength, for example carrying shopping and moving furniture. Lower back pain is often a result of poor lifting technique in everyday situations. The erector spinae muscles of the back need to be capable of applying enough force to offset the considerable load acting in an anterior direction on the facet joints and on the inter-vertebral discs during lifting. They need to be capable of holding the spine erect against the weight of a load pulling the body forwards.

Not only do the back muscles need to be strong when lifting, but the abdominal muscles also need to be strong enough to fixate the **vertebrae** and to prevent **hyper-extension** of the spine when carrying loads.

<table>
<tr><td>**DEFINITION**</td></tr>
</table>

Vertebrae are the individual bones that make up the spine.
Hyperextension refers to overextension of a joint.

The National Fitness Survey (1992)[3] reported very poor leg power in the UK, reflecting the trend in much of the western world. Without enough strength in the legs and trunk to enable you to bend down and lift correctly (with a straight back and bent knees) you risk damaging your back every time you pick up so much as a pencil or piece of paper from the floor.

Position statements from the US Surgeon General's Office, based on recent research world-wide, upholds strength training as the key factor in maintaining functional ability, health and independence as we age.[4]

Doesn't strength training reduce flexibility?

The range of movement (ROM) evident in Olympic weightlifters belies the myth that strength training reduces flexibility. As with most exercise much is dependent on how the exercise is carried out. If a full range of movement is used during strength work then a full range of movement will be maintained. Further, as functional flexibility is reliant not only on **passive range of movement** but also on **active range**, then strengthening exercises may be found to improve flexibility and counteract the potential for injury to the muscles and joints.

<table>
<tr><td>**DEFINITION**</td></tr>
</table>

Passive range of movement is demonstrated when joint movement is assisted by an outside force.
Active range of movement is the range of movement when only the muscles affecting that movement are used.

In a study on physical education students it was found that strengthening exercises did not significantly reduce the passive flexibility scores but were found to stabilise the joints by increasing the active ROM, thus reducing the difference between the active and passive ranges.[5]

<table>
<tr><td>**♦ Power ♦**</td></tr>
</table>

Power = speed x strength

Power is dependent on both force production and the rate at which that force can be produced.

Power is a product of the speed of contraction and force of contraction, with peak power output generally occurring at around 30% of maximum velocity (*see* figure 5.2). Dependent on an individual's power-generating capacity, application of peak power in the quadriceps may allow for that person to just manage to rise from their chair or may cause the person to leap into the air! For power athletes such as

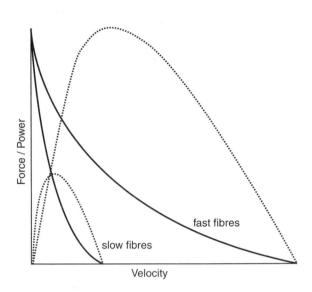

Figure 5.2 Force-velocity relationship of skeletal muscle in slow, and fast fibres. Power-velocity relationships are shown in broken lines (Taken from *Medicine and Sport Science* edited by M. Hebbelinck, Brussels; R.J. Shepphard, Toronto, Ont.)

sprinters, throwers, jumpers and Olympic weightlifters, a large number of fast twitch fibres capable of generating peak power quickly is therefore advantageous.

Multiple sprint sport athletes are characterised by an ability to keep repeating maximal sprint efforts with short recovery periods. The ability to recover quickly from, and reproduce, maximal efforts is more important to these athletes than maximal achievable power. Nevertheless, many world class team players would also make world class sprinters.

◆ Endurance ◆

Endurance is dependent on repeated sub-maximal intensity contractions. However, both type I and type IIA fibres are responsible for prolonged exercise of sub-maximal intensity, thus speed in endurance events requires that we train the type IIA fibres to utilise oxygen more efficiently and so accumulate less lactate. Therefore endurance cannot be considered only in terms of fibre type recruitment but must also be considered in metabolic terms.

Fatigue in endurance activity is partially a function of build up of lactate and partially due to the draining of muscle glycogen stores. Repleting the muscle glycogen stores may take as long as two days.

Endurance training increases the size and number of the mitochondria in both type I and type IIA muscle fibres, thus increasing the aerobic ability of the muscle and the ability to utilise fat as fuel. The ability of a muscle to use fat as fuel is related to the size and number of the mitochondria. This spares muscle glycogen stores in prolonged low-intensity exercise and also reduces lactate production thus prolonging the time to fatigue and facilitating higher intensity exercise without fatigue.[6, 7, 8]

◆ Can muscle fibre type be ◆ changed with training?

Each muscle or group of muscles has an associated nerve fibre which innervates the muscle to contract, and it is this nerve fibre which directs muscle fibre type. Only changing the nerve will change the fibre type. There is no conclusive evidence that it is possible to convert slow twitch fibres to fast twitch fibres, or fast twitch fibres to slow twitch through training. **Biopsies** of the muscles of élite endurance athletes show that they have almost no type IIB fibres, but have a significant percentage of type IIA fibres. Whether these athletes are born with a very high percentage of type IIA fibres and so are able to become élite endurance athletes, or whether endurance training over many years causes the type IIB fibres to transition into type IIA fibres is unclear.

DEFINITION

In **needle biopsies** a needle with a canula is inserted into the muscle tissue and a small piece of muscle tissue is withdrawn.

Endurance training at high intensities recruits the type I and type IIA fibres and loads them repeatedly, with little or no rest. The body responds by developing more mitochondria and more aerobic enzymes, and increasing the surrounding capillary network. High-intensity endurance training therefore trains the type IIA fibres to utilise oxygen in the aerobic production of energy. While this does nothing to enhance their maximum power output, it does increase sustainable power, allowing a higher intensity of exercise to be fuelled by aerobic respiration and reducing the build up of lactic acid.

Can I train to be a better sprinter?

Training for sprint and power sports loads all the fast twitch fibres for power.

INTEREST

During brief maximal exercise of five to six seconds duration, by using the creatine-phosphate system and the stored ATP, a power output of two to three times higher than at VO_2max can be achieved.[9]

- Muscle lactate increases by around 200%.

- Creatine-phosphate contributes to about 50% of ATP resynthesis.
- Glycolysis contributes about 50% of ATP resynthesis.

It is suggested that sprint training increases muscle use of creatine-phosphate and the enzymes associated with anaerobic metabolism, thus the type IIA fibres become well adapted for speed but not so well adapted for endurance.[10]

INTEREST

It may be possible to increase creatine-phosphate by supplementing the diet with creatine.[11, 12]

The muscle fibre does not distinguish between the force needed to lift a weight and the force needed to sprint or jump. It is simply innervated to contract and supply force, thus recruitment of fibres in sprint training may lead to greater muscle mass, which in turn may lead to greater power output and less fatigue during any given high power output.

♦ Are strength training and ♦ endurance training compatible?

The answer to this question depends upon:

- the type of strength and endurance training you are doing
- how well trained you already are
- what your exercise mode is *and*
- what you hope will be the outcome.

A large amount of scientific research has studied strength training alongside running and the results have been equivocal. [13, 14, 15, 16, 17]

The difficulty for researchers is that performance is multi-faceted rather than dependent on a single component, and that different people respond in different ways depending on their genetics, age, gender and training status.

Is strength training good for the endurance athlete?

Any increase in muscle mass, without a proportional increase in muscle oxidative capacity, might actually be viewed as detrimental to the performance of the endurance athlete. Thus research that measures VO_2max, mitochondrial density or the enzyme profile of the fibre types, draws the conclusion that strength training is detrimental to endurance, especially in activities such as running and cross country skiing where the body weight must be supported.

However, studies that use improved performance as their measure often conclude that improved strength is of benefit to the endurance athlete. This improvement in performance may be a function of greater sustainable power output, of improved mechanical efficiency or of fewer injuries. It would seem sensible that endurance athletes such as cross country skiers, rowers and paddlers who rely on either upper body muscle or a combination of upper and lower body muscle, would benefit from greater upper body strength. Certainly wheelchair marathoners rely on good upper body muscle mass and strength.

Is endurance training good for the strength athlete?

If increased strength is the aim of the athlete, endurance training of relatively short duration, such that it does not deplete glycogen stores, would seem to have no detrimental effect.

However, long duration training that thoroughly depletes the glycogen stores forces the body to utilise protein and break down muscle as an energy source and is therefore **catabolic** in nature. Thus this type of training may limit strength gains.

DEFINITION

Catabolism is the breaking down of muscle tissue – the destructive phase of metabolism. **Anabolism** is the building up of muscle tissue – the constructive phase of metabolism.

The strength–endurance continuum

Strength and endurance are not two separate issues, but rather a continuum of strength and endurance exists.

At one end of the continuum we have absolute strength, requiring maximum muscular force to be generated in one singular voluntary contraction. That is a force that will overcome a resistance once only, or in weight training terms the ability to lift a weight once only.

DEFINITION

1RM – one repetition maximum. The resistance needed to limit the lifter to one repetition only. A second repetition of the exercise cannot be achieved.

At the other end of the continuum is the ability to apply a muscular force repeatedly. This could be any number of contractions, and in endurance activities may be many hundreds of contractions. In strength training terms this end of the continuum would be represented by any number above 15 contractions (usually between 15RM and 25RM).

The strength end of the continuum represents activities with a high intensity, high force of contraction and great fatigueability.	This end of the continuum would recruit both slow and fast twitch muscle fibres, and would derive large amounts of its energy needs from anaerobic sources.	The endurance end of the continuum represents activities with low intensity, low force of contraction and less fatigueability.	This end of the continuum would recruit mainly slow twitch muscle fibres and would derive large amounts of its energy needs from aerobic sources.

STRENGTH
1RM

ENDURANCE

INTEREST

The changes in a muscle are specific to the stimulus placed upon it. If the stimulus is of low intensity and towards the endurance end of the continuum then the changes will be to the slow twitch muscle and will improve its endurance capabilities. If the stimuli are very high in intensity then they will involve the fast twitch muscle and will improve its strength capabilities.

Strength endurance crossover

If a muscle or group of muscles is extremely weak, such as after prolonged bed rest, then any activity, even if normally classified as an endurance activity, is likely to increase the strength capabilities of that group of muscles.

Likewise, as each motor unit becomes stronger, such as happens with heavy resistance training, then fewer motor units are needed to complete a given maximum workload, thus creating a greater motor unit reserve and increasing endurance capabilities.

1 Nelson, M.E. (1997) *Strong Women Stay Young.* Bantam Books

2 Stone, M.H., Fleck, S.J., Triplett, N.T. and Kraemer, W.J. *The health and performance related potential of resistance training.* Sports-Medicine. Vol. 11, no. 4

3 Allied Dunbar National Fitness Survey Report, April 1992

4 U.S. Department of Health and Human Services, Centers for Disease Control and Prevention, National Center for Chronic Disease Prevention and Health Promotion, (1996)

5 Barton, L., Bird, H.A., Lindsay, M., Newton, J. and Wright, V. (1995) *The effect of different joint interventions on the range of movement at a joint.* Journal of Orthopaedic Rheumatology (United Kingdom) 8/2, 87–92

6 Gollnick, P.D. and Saltin, B. (1982) *Significance of skeletal muscle oxidative enzyme enhancement with endurance training.* Clinical Physiology (England) 2/1, 1–12

7 Sidossis, L.S., Stuart, C.A., Shulman, G.I., Lopaschuk, G.D. and Wolfe, R.R. (1986) *Glucose plus insulin regulate fat oxidation by controlling the rate of fatty acid entry into the mitochondria.* Journal of Clinical Investigation (USA) 98/10

8 Abernethy, P.J., Thayer, R. and Taylor, A.W. (1990) *Acute and chronic responses of skeletal muscle to endurance and sprint exercise.* Sports Med. (New Zealand) 10/6, 365–89

9 Boobis, Williams and Wooton (1982) *Human muscle metabolism during brief maximal exercise.* Journal of Applied Physiology. 338: 21–2

10 Bogdanis, G.C., Nevill, M.E., Boobis, L.H. and Lakomy, H.K.A. (1996) *Contribution of phosphocreatine and aerobic metabolism to energy supply during repeated sprint exercise.* Journal of Applied Physiology (USA) 80/3

11 Greenhaff, P.L. (1995) *Creatine: its role in physical performance and fatigue and its application as a sports food supplement.* Insider. Vol 3, no 1

12 Dawson, B., Cutler, M., Moody, A., Lawrence, S., Goodman, C. and Randall, N. (1995) *Effects of oral creatine loading on single and repeated maximal short sprints.* Australian Journal of Science and Medicine in Sport (Australia) 27/3

13 Johnston, R.E., Quinn, T.J., Kertzer, R. and Vroman, N.B. (1995) *Strength training in female distance runners: impact on running economy.* Medicine and Science in Sports and Exercise 27(5), supplement abstract 47

14 Hortobagyi, T., Katch, F.I. and Lachance, P.F. (1991) *Effects of simultaneous training for strength and endurance on upper and lower body strength and running performance.* The Journal of Sports Medicine and Physical Fitness 31, 20–30

15 Blessing, D.L., Gravelle, B.L., Wang, Y.T. and Kim, C.K. (1995) *The influence of co-activation on the adaptive response to concurrent strength and endurance training in women.* Medicine and Science in Sports and Exercise 27(5), supplement

16 Gravelle, B.L. and Blessing, D.L. (1995) *Physiological adaptation in women concurrently training for strength and endurance.* Medicine and Science in Sports and Exercise 27(5)

17 MacDougall, J.D., Sale, D.G., Moroz, J.R., Elder, G.C.B., Sutton, J.R. and Howard, H. (1979) *Mitochondrial volume density in human skeletal muscle following heavy resistance training.* Medicine and Science in Sports 11, 164–6

Chapter 6

Aerobic Fitness

◆ Cardio-respiratory ◆ fitness

What is the difference between cardio-respiratory fitness and aerobic fitness?

The condition of the heart, circulation and lungs together make up cardio-respiratory fitness, that is how good the body is at extracting oxygen from the air, returning carbon dioxide to the air and pumping blood around the body. The heart is a muscular pump responsible for circulating blood around the body via a system of blood vessels. Arteries carry blood away from the heart, veins carry blood towards the heart, and an intricate network of fine capillaries and venules link the arteries with the veins.

The lungs are responsible for the exchange of gases between the body and the environment.

Cardio-vascular (CV) training is aimed at improving the efficiency of the pump, the heart. Aerobic fitness is also dependent on the condition of the working muscles and how well adapted they are to withdraw oxygen from the bloodstream and utilise it in aerobic respiration. Realistically, any improvement in cardio-vascular fitness in an untrained individual will be accompanied by improvements in the aerobic ability of the muscle, however, in highly trained individuals different types of training will target specific areas and help the athlete to achieve the best performance.

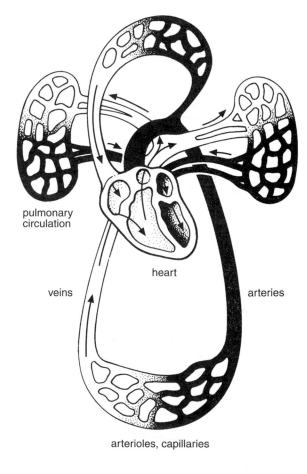

pulmonary circulation

heart

veins

arteries

arterioles, capillaries

Figure 6.1 The cardio-respiratory system

Is a slow heart rate good for me?

The bloodstream carries oxygen, carbon dioxide, fuel, hormones, enzymes, heat and waste products around the body.

There is a need for the body to regulate the speed of the pumping heart. With the onset of exercise, more oxygen is needed in the working muscles, there is more carbon dioxide to expel from the body, and excess heat must be dissipated, so a greater flow of blood must be pumped around the body.

As we exercise, therefore, there is an increase in heart rate (HR) in an attempt to supply oxygen to meet the extra demand, and to get rid of carbon dioxide from the working muscles. To assist the heart in this work the body is also able to regulate the internal dimensions of various blood vessels, constricting or dilating them in order to direct blood to the parts of the body where it is most needed while maintaining blood pressure.

INTEREST

- During rest about 5% of the blood pumped each minute is directed towards the skin. When exercising in a hot, humid environment, as much as 20% is directed towards the skin in an attempt to dissipate heat. As heat loss is via perspiration we need to ensure that we drink plenty while we exercise. If we do not then we will dehydrate, affecting our blood volume, blood pressure and ability to perform.
- Fluid loss can be measured by weight loss. A decrease of just 2% of your body weight equates to a decrease in performance of about 6–7%. A fluid loss of 5% of body weight equates to a decrease in performance of 30% and may result in nausea, vomiting and diarrhoea[1].

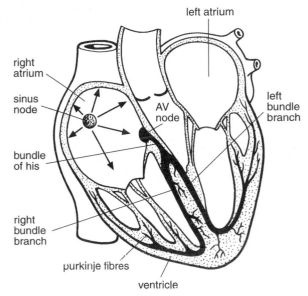

Figure 6.2 The heart's internal pacemaker

The heart has an internal pacemaker known as the sino atrial node (S-A node) which spontaneously polarises and depolarises to provide stimulation for the heart to contract.

This pacemaker activity is totally separate from the nervous system of the body, so the heart would continue to beat at 70–80 beats per minute (bpm) under the influence of the S-A node even if all nervous fibres were cut. There are, however, neural influences superimposed upon this inherent contractile rhythm.

Long term exercisers exhibit changes in these neural influences and this has the effect of slowing the heart rate at rest. Therefore, healthy regular exercisers have a slower resting heart rate than healthy non-exercisers. Equally, for any given sub-maximal workload the heart of a trained person will beat more slowly than in the untrained state.

Despite this they are still able to pump blood around the body effectively, because although the resting heart rate (RHR) is slower, there is more blood expelled from the heart with each beat, that is they have a greater stroke volume. Normally a small amount of blood, about 50–70ml remains in the left ventricle of the heart after the heart contracts. Training enhances the force of contraction such that a greater volume of blood is ejected from the heart at each stroke. This greater **stroke volume** increases the **cardiac output** dramatically. In fact, during maximum work, the highly trained endurance athlete has a cardiac output equal to twice that of his sedentary counterpart[2].

The increase in stroke volume may also be partly due to enhanced venous return, as the slower heart rate increases the time available for the heart to fill with blood. This increase in venous return during **diastole** stretches the wall of the heart, the myocardium, and in the same way that a stretched elastic band has more stored power, this causes a more powerful ejection stroke when the heart contracts.

Maximum exercise				
	heart rate x stroke volume		=	cardiac output
untrained person	195bpm x 113ml		=	22l
trained person	195bpm x 179ml		=	35l

♦ Respiratory system ♦

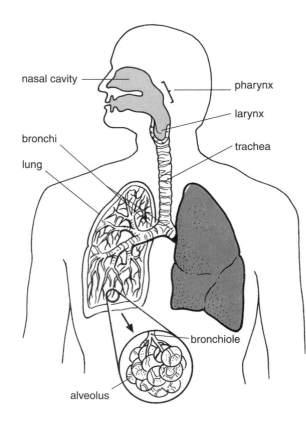

Figure 6.3 The respiratory system

The function of lungs is the exchange of gases between the internal environment of the body and the external environment. This gaseous exchange is achieved by utilising muscular bellows to draw air into the lungs and force air out. Inside the lungs are tiny little air sacs called alveoli, each made of a very thin semi-permeable membrane through which oxygen and carbon dioxide can pass. In the normal healthy adult there are more than 300 million of these little alveoli, with a total surface area equal to half the size of a tennis court but occupying a volume of only four to six litres, that is the amount of air in a basketball.

We breathe in air from which oxygen diffuses across the walls of the alveoli into the blood capillaries. Carbon dioxide from the blood diffuses across the walls of the alveoli into the air in the lungs and is breathed out.

What happens to the oxygen after it reaches the bloodstream?

The oxygen is carried in the bloodstream on the protein haemoglobin found in the red blood cells. When it reaches the working muscles it is given up by the haemoglobin and taken up by the muscles where it is transported to the mitochondria for use in aerobic production of energy.

As we exercise, the working muscles utilise oxygen and produce carbon dioxide, thus changing the concentration of both of these gases in the blood. This changes both the **concentration gradients** and the **partial pressures** of oxygen and carbon dioxide in the body.

DEFINITION

Concentration gradient. Gases diffuse from high concentration to low concentration along a concentration gradient.
Partial pressure is the pressure exerted by individual gases in a mixture of gases.

Why do I feel short of breath?

We are stimulated to breathe harder, not by a lack of oxygen in the bloodstream, but by an increase in carbon dioxide.

In an effort to get rid of the carbon dioxide we are stimulated to breathe out rather than to breathe in.

Ventilation rate is also affected:

• when stretch receptors in lung tissue fire an automatic response
• when there is an increase in internal body temperature
• when there is a fall in blood pressure
• when there is increased acidosis in the blood (as when there is a build up of lactic acid).

When the body is at rest the most important respiratory stimulus is carbon dioxide pressure in the bloodstream.

It is thought that in most healthy individuals the pulmonary system does not limit performance. However, in diseased lungs, or if the ability to breathe is inadequate, as is the case in people with asthma, it may be that aerobic capacity is limited by the failure of breathing to keep pace with the body's demand for oxygen.

The muscles that cause us to breathe, the diaphragm and intercostal muscles, utilise oxygen themselves to provide the energy for contraction.

In people with severely diseased lungs, the oxygen cost of breathing may reach as much as 40% of the total oxygen cost of exercising.

What effect does training have on the function of the lungs?

Training increases the number of capillaries surrounding the alveoli. This increased pulmonary capilliarization increases the ability of the lungs to exchange gases.

Because the diaphragm and intercostal muscles which control breathing are also trainable, regular exercise increases their ability to force air out of the lungs. Thus forced vital capacity, the amount of air that can be forced out of the lungs in one breath, is increased.

What effect does exercise have on the exchange of gases?

After only four weeks of training the amount of oxygen extracted from the air and utilised by the body is increased, independently of the amount of air being moved in and out of the lungs. Thus we don't have to breathe so hard to extract the same amount of oxygen from the air. This means that a smaller amount of air is breathed at any given sub-maximal workload, and the energy cost of breathing is thus reduced.

♦ Maximum aerobic ♦ capacity (VO$_2$max)

Maximum aerobic capacity (VO$_2$max) or aerobic power is the maximum amount of oxygen that you can extract from the air and utilise in the working muscles for the aerobic production of energy. In other words, how much oxygen you can use when exercising at very high intensities. VO_2max is affected by body size, gender and age, and is measured in litres/minute and often expressed relative to body weight, in ml/kg of body weight per minute.

1 McKardle, W., Katch, F. and Katch, V. *Exercise Physiology* (3rd edition). Lea and Febiger. Chapter 25
2 Wilmore, J. and Costill, D. *Physiology of Sport and Exercise*. Chapter 9
3 Astrand, P.O. and Rodahl, K. *Textbook of Work Physiology* (3rd edition). McGraw Hill. p. 333

INTEREST

Average VO_2max levels for women are about 65–70% of that of men. The mean value for a 65-year-old man is the same as that of a 25-year-old woman.[3]

VO_2max is trainable but has a genetic ceiling, i.e. you are born with a set limit on VO_2max. Very high values have been recorded in élite endurance athletes. The higher the VO_2max the more able that person is to utilise oxygen to fuel exercise, therefore the greater the potential for high level performance in endurance sports.

INTEREST

The average man has a VO_2max of 45ml/l/min., while average world class cross country skiers have a VO_2max of around 86.7ml/l/min.

Training can enhance VO_2max but only within that person's genetic ceiling. In other words, training can only help you to make the best use of the potential with which you were born.

The Principles of Fitness Training

Chapter 7

Goals

◆ Why are you training? ◆

Before you start planning your training, you need to work out why you are training.

QUOTE

'If you set a goal for yourself and are able to achieve it, you have won your race. Your goal can be:

- to come in first
- to improve your performance
- or just finish the race.

– it's up to you.'

DAVE SCOTT, TRIATHLETE

Around 50% of people who start exercising drop out in the first few months. Many of them never really understood why they started in the first place. They had a notion that it was good for them or that they 'ought to do something', but because they don't know what they want from exercising they don't achieve anything. When they stop they just accept defeat. 'I tried it but I couldn't do it'.

In order to put a training programme together in such a way that it will work, i.e. that you get maximum benefits from the time you spend training, you really need to have thought a little about what you want from the training programme. 'I just want to get fit' are words often heard by personal trainers and fitness coaches. This is fine if you know what you mean by fit.

A friend of mine once introduced me as 'the fittest person I know' which, though flattering, came at a time when I was recovering from a very debilitating bout of flu, following a very frustrating period of deconditioning due to lack of time in which to train. I certainly was not the fittest person that I knew. I was not fit at all when judged by my own standards, however by my friend's standards, even in my state of poor training, I was extremely fit.

Ask twenty different people what 'fit' is and you will get twenty different answers.

So you must ask yourself: 'What do I want from my training programme? What do I want the results to be?'

'I just want to stay fit'

Some people really do just like to be fit. It makes them feel good about themselves, it

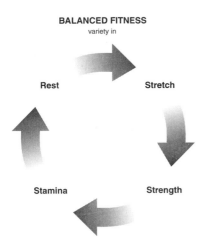

BALANCED FITNESS
variety in

Rest

Stretch

Stamina

Strength

Figure 7.1 Balanced fitness

helps them to stay looking good, and it means that when they go away for the weekend or on holiday they can take a sailboard out, go skiing, or just kick a football around without crippling themselves.

For these people writing a cross training programme is mostly about adding variety to their training and creating balance; changing something on a regular basis so that they don't get bored and ensuring that the programme provides balanced fitness so that they don't get injured and remain as healthy as possible.

For these people a combination of stretch, strength and stamina is the key. They may simply work on all of these all of the time, or they may concentrate more on one or other aspect at different times of the year. Variety, however, may be assured by writing a training programme that focuses on different disciplines at different times of the year.

For instance, one of my clients liked to do more strength work in the winter when it was cold and wet outside, and more endurance work in the summer when she liked to be outside in the sunshine. She would work on

| File | Edit | View | Print | | | | | | | | | Layer 1 | Layer 2 | Layer 3 | | | | R | Move | M |

Start Date												End Date
05-Jan-98					Macrocycle							**28-Dec-98**

Jan	Feb	Mar	Apr	May	Jun	Jul	Aug	Sep	Oct	Nov	Dec
5 12 19 26	2 9 16 23	2 9 16 23 30	6 13 20 27	4 11 18 25	1 8 15 22 29	6 13 20 27	3 10 17 24 31	7 14 21 28	5 12 19 26	2 9 16 23 30	7 14 21 28

Mesocycles

05-Jan-98	09-Mar-98	04-May-98	06-Jul-98	07-Sep-98	02-Nov-98
One	two	three	four	five	six
strength, flexibility and some CV work	strength, flexibility and increase CV	strength/endurance; increase CV work	endurance	increase strength again	strength, flexibility and some CV work
weights 3X week; swim 2Xweek; indoor row 1x week; stretch class 2 X week, plus stretch every session	weights 2Xweek; swim 1Xweek; run 2x week; cycle X1 week stretch class 1 X week, plus stretch every session	weights 2Xweek; run 3: week; cycle X2 week stretch every session	skate X2 week; run x 3; cycle x 1 stretch every session	weights x 2 week; run x 1; swim x 2, stretch class x 2	weights 3X week; swim 2X week; indoor row 1x week; stretch class 2 X week, plus stretch every session

Linked 31-Dec-1998 get fit
Goals.

*Figure 7.2 **The mesocycles in this training plan show the variety in training throughout the year***

stretch, strength and stamina all through the year, but during the winter would emphasise strength by spending time in the club, the pool, on the cardio-vascular machines and working with resistance equipment. During the summer she would be out on her bike or her rollerblades or running more, spending a minimum of time inside.

♦ 'SMART' goals for ♦ great rewards

Psychologists tell us that when we strive to achieve something we put more effort in if the rewards are greater. Unfortunately, where exercise is concerned, many of us haven't assimilated the rewards well enough to know how great or small they are.

To discover the rewards we need to be specific about the goal. It may be that if I win Wimbledon I will be able to stop worrying about my finances for the next year; it may be that if I finish the local triathlon my self esteem will be improved dramatically and I will no longer watch the finishers and think, I wish I had done that; it may be that if I include weight training in my cross training programme I am able to stabilise my shoulder joint and will then really go for the high brace in the kayak and won't capsize so often.

Whatever it is, if the rewards are great enough you will be more able to stick to the training plan and achieve your goals. To do this you must define your goals and define them accurately enough to prioritise them. Which one has the greatest reward?

Defining your goals accurately involves being SMART.

SMART goals are **S**pecific, **M**easurable, **A**greed, **R**ealistic and **T**imed.

Specific

If you really want to reach your goals, the more specific you make them the better. 'I want to get fit' could mean: I want to be able to walk to the shops and back without getting tired, or I want to run a marathon in under three hours. 'I want to look better' could mean: I want to lose some weight, or I want to put on some weight. Setting specific goals means that you have to define that goal as clearly as you can.

Measurable

A goal is better if it can be measured. 'I want to lose weight' could mean: I want to lose 7lbs, or it could mean my jeans are too tight and I want to be able to zip them up easily. 'I want to do the marathon' could mean: I want to run every step of the way, or I will be happy to get around with a combination of run and walk. However, if you can't measure your goal, how will you know when you have achieved it?

Agreed

If a goal is not your own goal you are not likely to have the motivation to achieve it. The rewards for you must be high. If a woman wants her husband to take more exercise in order to lose weight, but he is quite happy at his present weight, he is unlikely to adhere to an exercise programme or diet for long enough to make a difference. The goal must be agreed; you must 'own' your goals. The higher priority they are in your mind the more likely you are to achieve them. Find something that excites you.

Realistic

Your goal must be realistic if you are to achieve it.

- 'I have never run before and I do no fitness activity but I want to run a marathon in a month's time' is unrealistic.
- However, 'I am a good cyclist, my event is 50-mile time trialling, and although I don't presently run I want to run a marathon in a month's time' is much more realistic.
- 'I have never run before and I do no fitness activity but I want to run a marathon in 12 month's time' is also much more realistic.

Timed

If a goal has no deadline it can be put off indefinitely. Timed goals are achieved far more often than open-ended goals. Most sports oriented goals are time limited by the date set for the competition, however 'I would like to compete in an ironman triathlon sometime' is different to 'I am going to compete in the Ironman Triathlon at Telford on 6th June'. The second goal is much more likely to be achieved as there is now an urgency in taking steps towards achieving it.

♦ Mini goals ♦

Once you have clearly defined high priority goals you can work out a strategy for achieving them. Within this strategy you will be able to set sub-goals, each one leading you closer towards your ultimate goal.

Sub-goals are easier to focus on as they are more readily achievable. For instance, I want to compete in an adventure race that involves kayaking, climbing, orienteering and mountain biking. Out of these four events I am a

competent orienteer, a reasonable mountain biker, a passable climber, but have never been in a kayak in my life. My top priority is therefore to learn to kayak.

OPINION

That is a sub-goal, however it is not SMART.

- How good at kayaking do I have to be for this event?
- Is this river kayaking, sea kayaking or lake kayaking?
- Will I encounter white water?
- What grade of white water will I encounter?

Once I have discovered that this is river kayaking with grade 2 rapids I begin to understand what I have to achieve. It is specific, measurable and timed. I have to be competent to paddle 30km including grade 2 rapids by the date of the race.

Is it realistic or agreed?

Well, if I really want to do it then it becomes agreed. I probably won't know if it is realistic until I get into a boat and start to paddle. Then I will find out whether I am an utter incompetent or whether I can become reasonable at paddling by the date set.

Possible sub-goals therefore include:

- join a club and learn to paddle
- paddle regularly
- learn about paddling on moving water
- add in weight training to stabilise my previously injured shoulder joint
- learn to roll
- learn about white water
- check how far I have to paddle for the event
- build in a fitness programme to enable me to paddle this far.

Having set these milestones for paddling I can look at the rest of my training and make sure that I keep up my skill and fitness levels for the other events in the competition. I can add milestones for the other events.

For instance, there is a running section of 50km, so I must build my running up to that distance. The run section is off-road and is mountainous with very few footpaths. The terrain is alternately rocky, heather and peat hags. I need to train specifically to be able to run this type of terrain, therefore I add some fell races and a mountain marathon to my programme as sub-goals for running. I also need to improve not only my distance but also my ability to run up and down hills. Running hills takes increased strength both to add power for going up hill and to stabilise my knees while running down hill. Paddling also needs strength – upper body strength – so in preparation for the extra hill work and for the paddling I must build some strength work into my programme. As climbing and mountain biking also require upper body strength, an all-round strength base is good preparation for more specific training later in the plan.

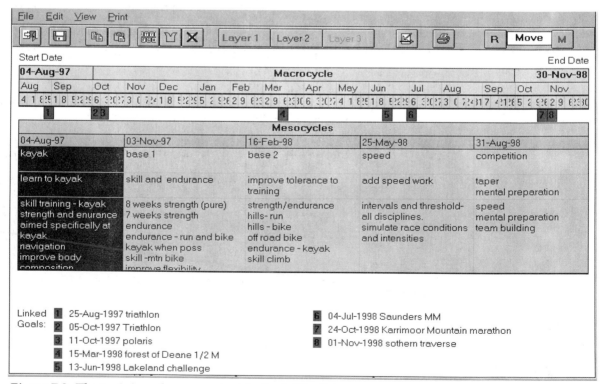

Figure 7.3 The training plan may start to look like this

♦ How do I plan for all ♦ of this?

I must now begin to build a plan to reach my long term goal.

How many competitions do I have to enter as mini goals?

The mini goals act as checkpoints to gauge how you are doing. They need not be competitions, they may be smaller goals, for instance if your goal is to lose a stone in weight a sub-goal may be to lose 7lbs. The mini goals may be fitness assessments or simply days on which you will try a particular challenge. You may choose a day to cycle a timed 25 miles; or to walk a set distance; or to try out certain of the events for an Ultrafit challenge in the gym.

OPINION

The mini goals show you that you are moving towards your major goal. If for the Ultrafit X-training challenge you need to bench press 40kg for 40 repetitions and previously you could only manage 30 repetitions, your mini goal may be to try for 40 repetitions. Now that you see that you can achieve this as an individual event, your next goal may be to combine it with some of the other events from the challenge.

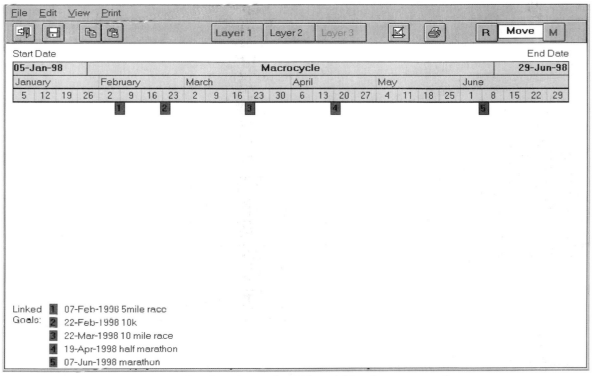

Figure 7.4 The above training plan has five sub-goals within the macrocycle

Mini goals also show you where you are in relation to where you want to be. If you were planning to compete in an Olympic distance triathlon and you knew that you had to have a run split of 42 minutes in the triathlon to achieve the overall time that you were aiming for, you may set a sub-goal of a 10km race. If running 42 minutes in this race was really tough just on its own, then you would know that running it at the end of a triathlon was going to be extremely tough.

DEFINITION

Taper. A reduction in training levels to ensure an athlete is fresh for a competitive event.

You need to keep in mind that mini goals are just that. You will not be race fit for your main goal at this time so you should not expect to achieve a personal best every time you go out. If the mini goals are races, you may not even **taper** but use them as a hard training session. It doesn't matter whether you could have raced better if you had tapered. You weren't meant to peak for this race. You will peak for your main race.

Once you have set your long term goal and your sub-goals you will know how much training time you have for the event. The period of time from now until you reach your main goal is called a macrocycle. You can split the macrocycle up into shorter sections during which you focus on particular elements of training. These shorter sections or phases are called mesocycles

You may have sub-goals scattered throughout the macrocycle. When setting sub-goals you should attempt to fit in where possible with the training mesocycles. For instance, if your training is geared towards triathlon and the run section of the race is 10km, you may look at improving your endurance in phase 1

and your speed in phase 2. Thus you may choose to run a 10-mile race as a sub-goal in phase 1, and 10km races during which you will concentrate on speed in phase 2.

OPINION

- The goals should be very personal.
- The SMART analogy helps to define goals accurately.
- Goals can be divided into major goals and sub-goals or mini goals.
- Mini goals mark how close you are getting to your major goal
- You may not want to peak for mini goals but use them to build towards your major goal.

Chapter 8

Training Principles

Having sorted out what you want from your training programme and what your training goals are, for training to be effective you need to follow a number of scientific principles.

OPINION

Writing a training programme involves manipulating:

Frequency
Intensity
Time
Type
Adherence

in such a way as to maximise the training benefits while encountering the minimum possible risk of injury or overtraining.

♦ Frequency ♦

Frequency relates to how often you train or exercise. If you are a single sport participant and you do not cross train at all, this refers to how often you exercise in total. If you run only, do you run three, five or six times a week?

If you cross train or are a multi-sport athlete this refers to how often you train in total and also how often you do each type of activity. For instance, for a triathlete this refers to how many times you swim, how many times you run, and how many times you cycle, and also how much this adds up to in total.

♦ Intensity ♦

Intensity of exercise refers to how hard you exercise. Single sport athletes who use only one exercise modality in their training alternate hard and easy sessions to reduce the stress on the body. When cross training is introduced into a programme it is possible to work hard on consecutive days because different activities are being used in training. However, even when cross training, it is best where possible to alternate hard and easy sessions, thus on one day a hard running session may combine with an easy bike session, or a hard swimming session may combine with an easy run session.

With resistance work, intensity is very often measured as a percentage of the total resistance that you could overcome, the total weight that you could lift for just one lift.

♦ Time ♦

Time relates both to the time spent exercising at each session and to the rest intervals. If the exercise session is a two-hour weights session in which 45 minutes is spent lifting and 95 minutes is spent resting, then the session time is 45 minutes. Low-intensity work, fuelled almost entirely by aerobic metabolism, can be maintained for long periods of time, while high-intensity work relies more heavily on anaerobic energy supplies and can be maintained for shorter periods of time.

During high-intensity work the total work time at that intensity can be increased by performing intervals of high-intensity work with low-intensity recovery periods. Thus an intensity that could only be maintained for 10 minutes in one session may be split into one-minute work intervals with two-minute rest intervals, thus allowing, say, 15 work intervals to be completed. The total work time at this intensity is therefore increased.

◆ Type ◆

Type relates to the type of training – is it weight training, swimming, running or cycling? Is it skill training, as in batting practice for cricket or paddle technique in kayaking? Is it strength work, long slow distance or speed work, intervals, fartlek, reaction time or flexibility training? All of these types interlink with frequency, intensity and time to complete the jigsaw.

◆ Adherence ◆

Only consistent training gives results. Every athlete misses some days of training due to overtiredness, illness, overwork, social occasions, etc. A few missed sessions are not too much of a problem as long as we get right back on track and start to train again. A cross training programme has the benefit of assisting with adherence by combating boredom and by providing a way of maintaining fitness during injury. By changing the emphasis of the programme it is possible to work around an injury.

◆ Progressive overload ◆

The body only adapts to unaccustomed demand. In other words you must overload to improve. However, if you cease to apply a training stimulus the acquired training adaptations will disappear. Overload must be progressive, and in order to progress you have to overload again before the training adaptations have disappeared. You have to stick with the programme in order to see results.

◆ SAID principles ◆

For fitness and sportspersons interested in specific improvements in performance, frequency, intensity, time and type must be manipulated within the SAID principle.

SAID stands for Specific Adaptation to Imposed Demand. That is, the physiological adaptation of the body depends entirely on the demand placed upon it.

OPINION

When weight training, if you train only the chest and biceps then only the chest and biceps will show increased strength and muscle hypertrophy. If you only run then all the physiological adaptations will be endurance-based rather than strength-based. However, the distinction is more subtle than this.

Training for sport must work towards improving the weak link in performance of that sport if overall performance is to improve.

A very skilful ice hockey player will play well at the start of a game but, without the endurance to last, will not play well at the end, while a very fit but less skilful player may play at the same mediocre level through-

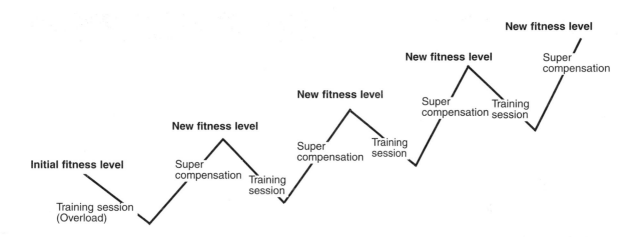

Figure 8.1 Super compensation due to overload during training: whenever a training session occurs and the system is overloaded the body reacts by adapting so it is able to cope with the stress of the training. In the process of adapting, the body super compensates such that it is able to cope if the stress of the next training session is greater. In this way, repeated bouts of unaccustomed stress through training, followed by enough recovery to allow for super compensation, results in an overall increase in fitness levels

out the whole game. The skilful player needs to work on fitness; skill will not help them once fatigue sets in. The fit player needs to work on skill. Further fitness improvements will not make them a better player.

The skilful player has the option of improving strength, muscular endurance, aerobic capacity, anaerobic power, anaerobic endurance. Where and how do they start? If they decide to work out in the gym, dependent on the type of workout they do they may improve muscular strength or muscular endurance. Which of these is going to improve their game most? If they decide to run, they may improve aerobic endurance. Will that help with a high-intensity multiple sprint sport? Do they need to improve anaerobic endurance? Can they improve one without the other? Won't weight training improve their anaerobic endurance? Taking a haphazard approach to training will give haphazard results.

The sports performer needs to analyse their game, their strengths and weaknesses and prioritise their workout accordingly. Let's say our ice hockey player lacks the ability to skate across the ice at speed. Is this because of lack of skating skill or is it a lack of power? If it is a lack of power then specific power drills may help. It may then be that ability to develop power is limited by a lack of strength, so building specific strength may need to precede the building of power. Having increased power the skater may now need to change their training to increase anaerobic endurance in order that those bursts of power last for longer. Anaerobic recovery may then allow those power bursts to be repeated sooner. An aerobic base may allow recovery to be repeated constantly throughout the match.

Perhaps more subtly still, different intensities of training will elicit a different physiological response. Thus running at 60% of VO_2max will give a different response to running at 70–80% VO_2 max, which will give a different response to running at 80–90% VO_2max.

FACT

Training at 60% of maximum heart rate will tax a different energy system and therefore elicit a different response in a deconditioned individual than in a well conditioned individual.

Likewise, changing a weight training system, for example the amount of weight lifted as a percentage of total ability, and even the order in which the exercises are carried out, will invoke a different training response.

Given all of this, what should the player concentrate on when they start training for improved fitness? Remember: Specific Adaptation to Imposed Demand. Clearly a structured approach to training is necessary.

♦ Rest ♦

To benefit most from fitness training, whether for improved health or improved performance, adequate rest is vital. Rest includes sleep time, relaxation time or simply non-training time. The quality of rest is also important. Dr. Heinz Liesen, national team doctor for the German soccer team during the World Cup finals of 1986 and 1990, discovered that football players spend the rest time between training sessions lying around and watching television. He therefore decided to increase their mental creativity by helping them to study new languages, hand crafts, and history, generally keeping their minds active both during training and during competition. The modestly talented German teams reached the World Cup final both in 1986 and 1990. Dr Liesen believes that both exercise level and creative mental activity are potential modulators of health and performance.

QUOTE

'In today's world of élite sport, the real limitation to continued improvement has moved from the quantity of training to the capacity of the mind and body for restitution. Many élite athletes are training 50 weeks per year, sometimes three to four hours per day. When this extreme physical stress is combined with the stress of more frequent competitions to satisfy sponsors, media pressure and a tendency to lose time or interest in mentally diverting creative activities, the results are often disastrous. What we often see if we observe closely is the sudden appearance of extremely talented performers, followed one or two years later by a decline in their performance or a complete disappearance from the scene. Behind these early burnouts is usually a coach or performance team that is pushing too hard.'
DR STEPHEN SEILER – *THE MIND BODY LINK*, MAPP
http://www.krs.hia.no/~stephens/brnbody.htm

OPINION

Include at least one rest day per week during which you rest completely or simply stretch.

♦ Nutrition ♦

If the body is to work at peak performance then it must have adequate fuel.

Good nutrition is vital to both training and performance. Deficiency of any group of nutrients can cancel out your best efforts in both training and performance. It is recommended that we eat a varied diet so as to provide all the vitamins, minerals and trace elements we need. Adding the physical stress of training to everyday life emphasises this need.

Chapter 9

Frequency

◆ Frequency ◆

The frequency with which you train has an impact on your recovery from and your adaptation to training. Training too often is detrimental as it does not allow your body enough time to adapt to the stresses placed upon it. Training too infrequently allows for retrogression to occur before the next training stimulus is applied and so no progress is made.

OPINION

Training for aerobic fitness should occur a minimum of three times per week and training for strength should occur a minimum of twice per week.

When training for a sport rather than for general fitness, depending on factors such as level of competition, training three times a week may not be enough, indeed many multi-sport athletes train more than once a day. For single sport athletes the danger of training daily or more than once a day comes from the risk of overuse injury.

In cross training this danger is reduced. The muscles are used slightly differently when running compared to when cycling, and the stress on the joints is different, therefore the injury risks from running three times and cycling three times in a week are less than from running six times, yet the cardio-vascular benefits may be equal. Similarly, running

four times a week and weight training twice a week may include less risk than running five times a week. Although the total number of training sessions is greater, the change in use and the strengthening of the muscles may increase the ability to maintain joint integrity during fatiguing run sessions and so reduce the potential for injury.

How often should I train?

This depends on:

- what your goals are
- how experienced you are
- your health history
- your injury history
- your age
- how much time you have available.

Health guidelines suggest that we should do 30–60 minutes of moderate intensity activity most days of the week in order to maintain or improve our health. Fitness guidelines suggest that we should do 20–30 minutes of vigorous aerobic activity three times per week plus two sessions of resistance type training in order to maintain or improve fitness. Of course, if your goals are performance related these guidelines may not apply.

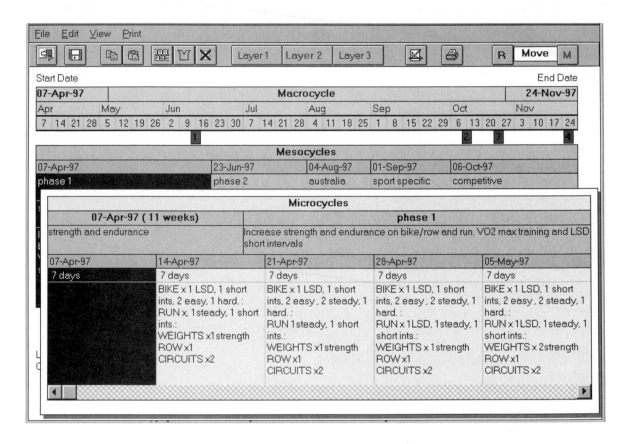

Figure 9.1 If you cross train or are a multi-sport athlete, frequency refers to how often you train in total and how often you do each type of activity

What are your goals?

If your goal is to complete an ironman triathlon, you will need to train more often and for longer than if you want to complete a sprint triathlon. For the ironman triathlon you may need to train more than one discipline per day, while for the sprint triathlon it is feasible that you may swim one day, cycle the next, run the next and so on. However, if your goal is to complete a sprint triathlon you are likely to have to train more often than if you want to simply complete a 10km run. For the triathlon you may train six days a week, whereas for the 10 km run you may only need to train for four or five days a week. Of course, if you want to excel at a 10km run, to be the best that you can be, then you may have to train more often than the person who simply wants to finish in the sprint triathlon. You may train six days a week and they may run one day, cycle one day and swim one day, i.e. three days training per week.

Do you have a history of injury?

If you have a history of injury you may need to either increase or decrease your training. It is likely that at first you will need to decrease training in the mode that caused the injury and give the injured area time to heal. This need not involve stopping training however. Instead you may run instead of row, or cycle instead of run, such that the injured area is rested but central fitness is maintained.

Subsequently, it may be that you add in specific strength and flexibility work, extra skill work, body awareness or proprioceptive training in order to strengthen the injured area and prepare for the rigors of training and competition with minimal risk of reinjury. For example, after a shoulder injury that occurred when crashing my mountain bike, I first reduced my training, cutting out most of my shoulder work in the gym, but after initial healing time I added backstroke swimming to my programme in order to work on strength and active flexibility and range of movement. This involved extra training over and above my norm.

How old are you?

Older athletes may be more prone to injury and may need to vary their training more. For example, run less frequently but add in cycling or rowing as extra endurance training. Their bodies may tolerate training as frequently as any other athlete so long as they vary the training mode.

Younger athletes with immature bone and soft tissue development will be injury prone if exposed to high training volumes. They may be able to train often but for shorter periods of time.

How much time do you have available?

One of the most important issues in training frequency is the time available. Planning to train twice a day will only lead to demotivation if this is a totally unrealistic time schedule for you to achieve. Thus even if training twice a day is optimal there is no point in planning this if it won't fit into your lifestyle. Remember when you plan time that you have to fit in showering, changing and eating if you are going to train effectively. Therefore if you can only take a one-hour lunch break and you plan for an hour's exercise, you will be late back to work and will not have eaten. Take this into account and plan realistically so that you don't disappoint and demotivate yourself.

Chapter 10

Intensity

♦ Intensity ♦

The intensity of exercise will depend on what you want to gain from it. Exercises simply to benefit health need not be performed at such a high intensity as is necessary when training for sports performance. As training at different intensities elicits a different training response, always working at the same intensity limits the adaptations made.

OPINION

Where possible, alternate hard and easy sessions, e.g. a hard running session may be followed by an easy bike session; a hard swimming session may be followed by an easy run session.

Training at high intensity puts tremendous stress on the body, both physiologically and psychologically, thus single sport athletes who use only one exercise modality in their training should alternate hard and easy sessions.

Cross training allows for high-intensity sessions on consecutive days because of the different nature of the stresses from the different activities used.

Below is an example of a cross training programme using different intensities in different disciplines. Friday is essentially a rest day though the client concentrates on stretching. Wednesday is an easy day with two easy sessions. Every other day has one hard session and one either easy or steady session in a different discipline. Thus hard and easy sessions are alternated each day, and for all disciplines except weight training.

How do I know what the intensity is?

During aerobic exercise heart rate increases in line with exercise intensity and with oxygen consumption and is therefore often measured as percentage of maximum heart rate or of VO_2max. However, during short, high-intensity intervals of less than three minutes, or during resistance exercise such as weight

Day	Activity a.m.	Intensity	Activity p.m.	Intensity
Monday	Swim	hard	Cycle	steady
Tuesday	Weight train	hard	Run	easy
Wednesday	Swim	easy	Circuit class	easy
Thursday	Row	steady	Cycle	hard
Friday	Rest		Stretch	
Saturday	Run	easy	Weight train	hard
Sunday	Cycle	easy	Run	hard

training or circuit training, heart rate is not a good indicator of work intensity.

OPINION

Note that percentage of maximum heart rate is largely irrelevant during weight training activity.

With resistance work, intensity is very often measured as a percentage of the total resistance that you could overcome, the total weight that you could lift for just one lift.

How do I know what my maximum heart rate is?

Maximum heart rate is most often estimated as 220 minus your age. Thus for a person who is 35, their maximum heart rate would be estimated as 185 beats per minute (220 − 35 = 185). Therefore, if they were to work at 75% of maximum heart rate they would work at around 139 beats per minute. This is often used for prescribing exercise intensity.

The formula of 220 minus your age is only an estimate of maximum heart rate. In reality maximum heart rate can be as much as 20 beats either side of this figure. Also, because different activities involve different body positions and different muscle mass, maximum heart rate varies with different activities. Maximum heart rate during activities that involve mainly upper body muscle mass such as kayaking is less than during those activities such as cycling that involve the large muscles of the legs. During cycling, body position will make a difference to the heart rate, cycling on the drops resulting in a slightly lower heart rate than sitting upright, irrespective of wind resistance.

True, maximum heart rate is the maximum heart rate at which a person can work. Thus because maximum heart rate in a kayak would be different to that during swimming, which would be different to that during running etc., the maximum values for the different activities are called peak heart rate. For multi-sport athletes or for cross training therefore, the peak heart rate for each different type of exercise in the training programme should be used to calculate heart rate at prescribed intensity for each different exercise modality.

Is my maximum heart rate the same as my VO_2max?

The heart rate at a given percentage of VO_2max is usually about 10 beats per minute lower than the same percentage of maximum heart rate. Thus at 60% VO_2max the heart rate is about 70% of maximum heart rate etc. This remains so until fairly high percentages of VO_2max are reached when the percentage of maximum heart rate and VO_2max become closer and finally converge at 100%.

Another, and possibly more accurate, way of using heart rate for prescribing exercise intensity for fit individuals is to use the Karvonen formula which calculates the percentage of maximum heart rate reserve. This correlates much more closely to the percentage of VO_2max.

If possible, when using the Karvonen formula the true peak heart rate and true resting heart rate should be used. Resting heart rate (RHR) is taken in the morning after waking up (gently), emptying the bladder and then resting again for a few minutes to allow the heart rate to settle.

To work out the heart rate for a given intensity of exercise then, take resting heart rate from peak heart rate for that type of exercise. This gives the maximum heart rate reserve (MHRR). Finally, decide on the percentage at which you wish to work, take that percentage of heart rate reserve and add on resting heart rate. This gives the target heart rate.

For example:

- my resting heart rate is 48bpm
- my peak heart rate during running is 193bpm
- my heart rate reserve when running is therefore 145 (193 − 48 = 145)
- if I want to work at 60% of VO_2max I would then take 60% of 145 (MHRR) and add 48 (RHR), giving me a target heart rate of 135bpm.
- my peak heart rate during road cycling is 185bpm
- my heart rate reserve when cycling is therefore 137bpm (185 − 48 = 137)
- 60% of my VO_2max when cycling is 60% of 137 + 48 = 130bpm. Five beats lower than during running.

How do I measure my heart rate?

To measure your heart rate you either need to palpate your pulse, usually done at the carotid artery on the neck or the radial artery on the wrist, or use a heart rate monitor which detects your heart rate, displays it and may also store it. The first method is highly inaccurate, as it is very difficult to monitor the pulse during exercise. The second is much more accurate, depending on the accuracy of the monitor used.

How do I know what my peak heart rate is?

Peak heart rate is maximum heart rate possible for an individual during any given exercise modality.

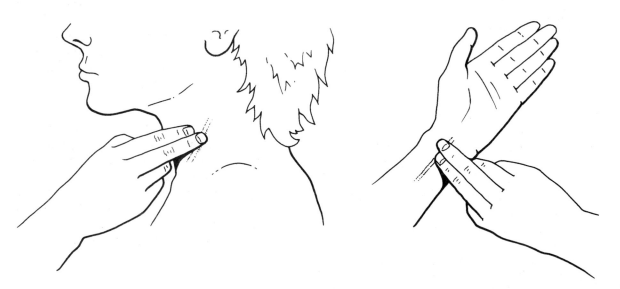

Carotid pulse

Radial pulse

Figure 10.1 Monitoring heart rate

To find your definitive peak heart rate, or maximum heart rate, you need to work to maximum while monitoring heart rate. In the laboratory this is done using ECG equipment, a resuscitation trolley and trained medical staff to monitor the subject, who exercises on an **ergometer** with increasing workloads. The heart rate and the workload will rise in a linear fashion until a point at which the heart rate plateaus or may even fall slightly. At this point the maximum heart rate has been reached. The workload may increase further for a short period of time, anaerobic metabolism being responsible for the increased energy production and power output beyond maximum heart rate.

DEFINITION

An **ergometer** is a piece of equipment which is calibrated and produces measurable units of work such that a person's work output can be measured.

INTEREST

The ACSM guidelines for apparently healthy individuals are as follows.

- 'Apparently healthy individuals can begin moderate (intensities of 40–60% VO_2max) exercise programmes (such as walking or increasing usual daily activities) without the need for exercise testing or medical examination, as long as the exercise programme begins and proceeds gradually and as long as the individual is alert to the development of unusual signs or symptoms.
- Moderate exercise is further described as being well within the individual's current capacity and can be sustained comfortably for a prolonged period, i.e. 60 minutes.

- Vigorous exercise (intensity > 60% VO_2max) is intense enough to represent a substantial challenge and results in significant increases in heart rate and respiration. Vigorous exercise usually cannot be sustained by untrained individuals for more than 15–20 minutes.
- At or above age 40 for men and aged 50 for women, it is desirable for individuals to have a medical examination and a maximal exercise test before beginning a vigorous exercise programme.
- At any age the information gathered from an exercise test may be useful to establish an effective and safe exercise prescription. Maximal testing for men at age 40 or above and for women at age 50 or above, even when no symptoms or risk factors are present, should be performed with physician supervision.
- Sub-maximal exercise testing up to 75% of age-predicted maximal heart rates in apparently healthy individuals of any age can be done without physician supervision if the testing is carried out by well trained individuals who are experienced in monitoring exercise tests and in handling emergencies.'

Thus any type of maximum exercise test should only be carried out with apparently healthy, asymptotic individuals who are used to regular high-intensity exercise.

One practical method of obtaining a working figure for peak heart rate is to monitor heart rate during a race situation when the subject is aiming to perform their best.

Do I have to measure heart rate?

Measuring heart rate is not always practical or desirable. Intensity can also be measured subjectively using a scale of perceived exertion or rate of perceived exertion (RPE). Borg's scale of perceived exertion (*see* right) rates the intensity of exercise between 6 and 20. For example, if the exercise feels 'somewhat hard' a score of 13 is given. This is said to be equivalent to a heart rate of 130 beats per minute.

In reality the heart rate during 'somewhat hard' exercise would depend on:

- that person's maximum heart rate
- their fitness level and training status
- whether they were used to intensive exercise
- what they had been doing in the previous day's training sessions
- the time of day
- the environmental temperature and humidity
- their nutritional state.

There are various type of field tests which aim to provide information on maximum heart rate, VO_2max and OBLA for individuals without access to a laboratory (*see* page 152).

However, it should be noted that with all exercise there is some risk. With maximum effort exercise, as used for these types of tests, the risk is dramatically increased.

Thus RPE is very useful in determining how hard a person is working relative to that day's conditions. For instance, one athlete who was training for an indoor rowing championship, could normally maintain a heart rate of around 180bpm for 3,000m on a Concept II rowing machine. He would normally rate this as a 'very hard' activity.

One weekend he ran the Karrimor International Mountain Marathon, an event which involved him running over rough, mountainous country, carrying a pack, for a

The Borg scale of perceived exertion

'How does the exercise feel?' rating:	
	6
very very light	7
	8
very light	9
	10
fairly light	11
	12
somewhat hard	13
	14
hard	15
	16
very hard	17
	18
very very hard	19
	20

Rating x 10 is approximately equal to the heart rate (e.g. somewhat hard = 13 x 10 = 130bpm). This scale works on the degree of exertion that a person feels.

total of 9.5 hours over two days. He rested the following two days and on the third day he rowed. He found it difficult to maintain a heart rate of 174bpm for 1,000m. He rated this session as 'very very hard'.

The micro trauma in his leg muscles sustained from the marathon had just not recovered enough for him to be able to sustain a power output that would allow for a heart rate as high as he could normally achieve on the rowing machine. Despite this, RPE was very accurate with regard to how intense that exercise session was in relation to his condition on that day.

Is 6 to 20 the only scale of perceived exertion?
Working on a scale of 6 to 20 can be difficult.
Many people find it easier to work on a scale
of 0 to 10, or 1 to 5.

0 to 10 points scale	
nothing at all	0
very very light	0.5
very light	1
light	2
moderate	3
somewhat heavy	4
heavy	5
	6
very heavy	7
	8
	9
very very heavy	10

This 0 to 10 scale is useful as a general tool to
focus people on how much effort they are
putting into their exercise.

For endurance athletes who need to balance
the intensity of different workouts more care-
fully in order to improve endurance performance, a 1 to 5 scale similar to one developed
by Tudor Bompa works well. Bompa
described a scale of 1 to 5 with the perception
of the intensity corresponding to a range of
percentage of MHR.

I have found that expanding the descrip-
tions can also be useful. For example, at level
1 I may feel I would be able to keep going for
hours; at level 2 I may be able to manage say
an hour; level 3 is an intensity that I could
maintain for 30–45 minutes; level 4 I could not
do for more than 15–20 minutes; and I just
don't like doing level 5 but will keep it up for
5–10 minutes if I have to. How well you can
cope with any of these levels is partly dependent on your level of training – highly trained
endurance athletes may maintain level 4 for
far longer than 20 minutes, while some top
level marathon runners are known to run
most of the marathon at threshold level.

Level	Description	MHR%
1	Easy aerobic	60–70
2	Steady moderate 1	71–75
3	Steady moderate aerobic 2	76–80
4	Anaerobic threshold (hard)	81–90
5	Maximal (very hard)	91–100

(Aerobic training intensities adapted from Bompa (1989))

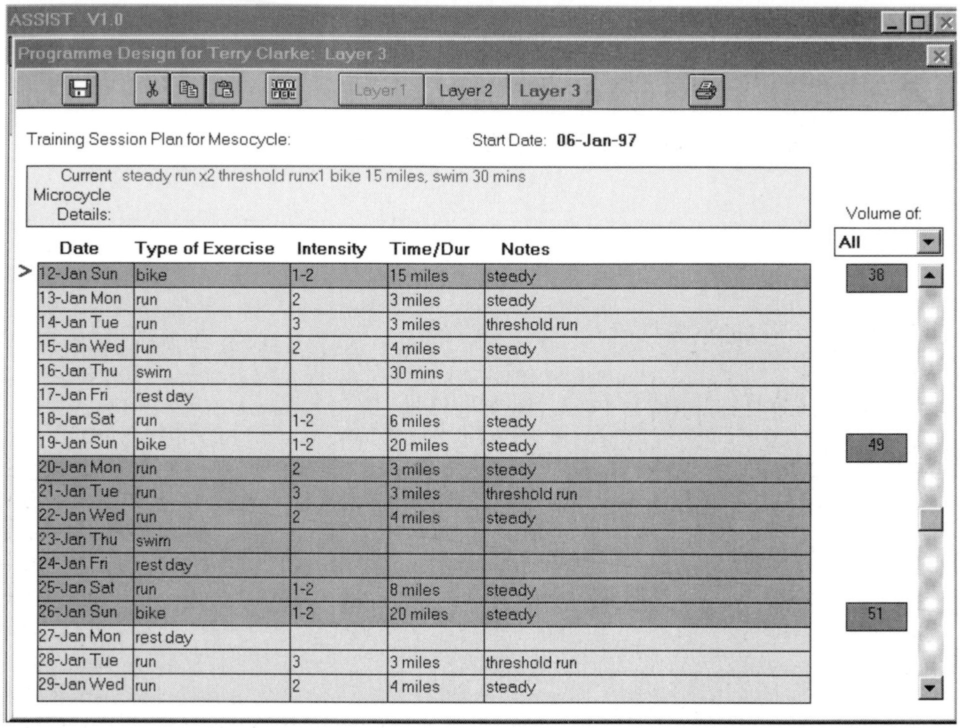

Date	Type of Exercise	Intensity	Time/Dur	Notes
12-Jan Sun	bike	1-2	15 miles	steady
13-Jan Mon	run	2	3 miles	steady
14-Jan Tue	run	3	3 miles	threshold run
15-Jan Wed	run	2	4 miles	steady
16-Jan Thu	swim		30 mins	
17-Jan Fri	rest day			
18-Jan Sat	run	1-2	6 miles	steady
19-Jan Sun	bike	1-2	20 miles	steady
20-Jan Mon	run	2	3 miles	steady
21-Jan Tue	run	3	3 miles	threshold run
22-Jan Wed	run	2	4 miles	steady
23-Jan Thu	swim			
24-Jan Fri	rest day			
25-Jan Sat	run	1-2	8 miles	steady
26-Jan Sun	bike	1-2	20 miles	steady
27-Jan Mon	rest day			
28-Jan Tue	run	3	3 miles	threshold run
29-Jan Wed	run	2	4 miles	steady

Figure 10.2 Intensity level is different on different days of training

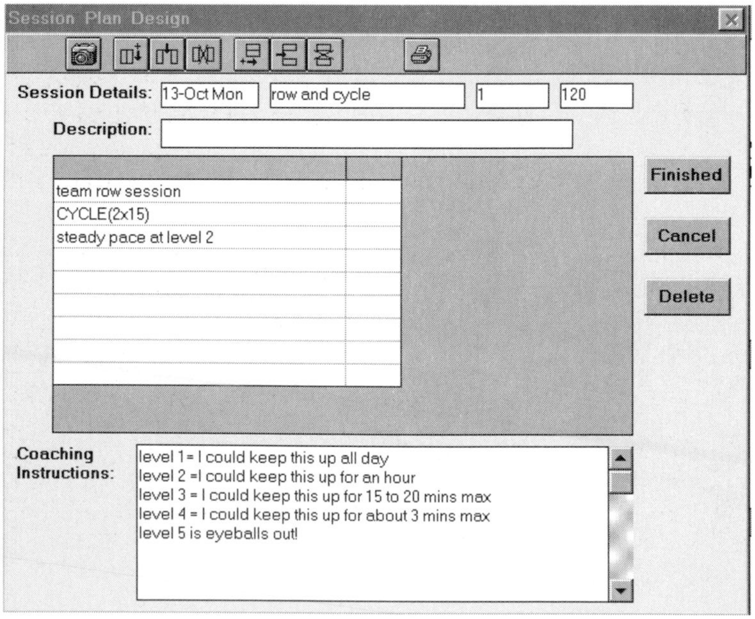

Figure 10.3 Expanding the description of intensity levels may be useful

Chapter 11

More About Intensity

◆ At what intensity should ◆ I train?

OPINION

Training intensity depends on:

- the physiological demands of the sport
- the aim of the training sessions
- the training status of the athlete
- the nutritional status of the athlete
- the health status of the athlete
- the age of the athlete
- the time available to train
- the season (time of the year).

The physiological demands of the sport

A sport that is very long duration, such as ultra distance running, demands high levels of endurance at a relatively moderate intensity. Another running sport, such as 1,500m running, also demands endurance but for a shorter period of time and at very high intensity. Different sports, in fact different disciplines within the same sport, and even different playing positions in team sport, make different physiological demands on the body. Thus the sport itself will demand a greater or lesser percentage of high-intensity training, and a greater or lesser percentage of low-intensity training.

When determining the physiological demands of a sport, the intensity and duration of exercise in the sport will help determine fibre type recruitment and the demands

Duration of exercise	Fuel	Energy supply
1–4 seconds	ATP	Anaerobic alactic
4–20 seconds	ATP+CP	Anaerobic alactic
20–45 seconds	ATP+CP+ muscle glycogen	Anaerobic alactic + Anaerobic lactic
45 seconds–2 minutes	muscle glycogen	Anaerobic lactic
2 minutes–4 minutes	muscle glycogen	Aerobic + Anaerobic lactic
4 minutes upwards	muscle glycogen + fatty acids	Aerobic

(Adapted from Jansen (1987))

Anaerobic alactic energy supply is anaerobic in nature but does not involve a build up of lactic acid (see page 88).

on the energy systems, which in turn will determine the emphasis of training.

Training status of the athlete

Dependent on the training status of the athlete, a different physiological response will be required. For instance, a detrained individual will make huge improvements by increasing their cardiac output and thus their VO_2max. However, an athlete who is training regularly may have reached their genetic limits in terms of their central circulation, but could make further improvements by concentrating on stimulating change at a cellular level, i.e. improving the number and size of the capillaries supplying the working muscle and the number and size of the mito-chondria in the muscle fibres. Thus while a beginner or a detrained individual may well benefit from doing most of their training between 60% and 90% of VO_2max, a trained individual will benefit from varying the training intensities.

Many superb endurance athletes concentrate on low- to moderate-intensity exercise for much of their training. In the world of distance running the Kenyan team are renowned. Studies by the exercise physiologist Bengt Saltin in 1995 showed that the Kenyan's did not have a superior VO_2max but that they accumulate less lactate than other athletes at any given intensity. His work revealed that large percentages of the Kenyan runners' training is completed at low to moderate intensities, under 75% VO_2max, but that they train at a variety of intensities.

	%VO₂max	%MHR	Adaptations	Energy systems	Fibre type recruitment
low intensity				Aerobic	Slow twitch
	55–65%	60–70%	Cardio-vascular function Fluid balance Substrate availability		
	65–85%	70–90%	Cardio-vascular function Mitochondrial density Capillary density	Aerobic	Type IIA
	85–100%	90-100%	Mitochondrial density Capillary density Lactate tolerance	Anaerobic glycolysis	
	>100%	N/A	Maximum force generation Lactate tolerance	Anaerobic glycolysis PCr	
high intensity					Fast twitch

Note that the adaptations taking place during training are complex and multi-faceted. The above table suggests only towards which end of the continuum between low intensity and high intensity different energy systems predominate, fibre type recruitment takes place and adaptations may be assumed to occur.

Further, dependent on the training status of the athlete, training at the same relative intensity will elicit a different metabolic and hormonal response. That is the hormonal and metabolic responses to exercise differ between fit and unfit individuals.[1]

Training intensity continuum

Physiological adaptations run along a continuum from low-intensity to high-intensity training. Where on the training continuum those physiological changes take place is partly dependent on the genetic inheritance of the athlete, and partly on the training status of the athlete. For instance, training at a heart rate equal to 85% of VO_2max will for one athlete be right on the limit of the anaerobic threshold and for another athlete be below the anaerobic threshold.

> **FACT**
>
> For deconditioned individuals, training at 60% VO_2max may be crossing the anaerobic threshold.

To reach their potential most athletes will have to do some training at all levels. How much training is spent at different intensities depends on the demands of the sport and the limiting factor in the athlete's performance.

The nutritional status of the athlete

It is known that high-intensity exercise relies on carbohydrate supplies, thus an athlete who does not eat enough carbohydrate will not be able to support high-intensity exercise. Likewise, an athlete who is dehydrated will struggle with a higher than normal heart rate and lower stroke volume, and higher than normal rate of perceived exertion for any given intensity level.

The health status of the athlete

High-intensity training is very fatiguing. It is known that the immune system is disrupted for a period from several hours to several days after a single bout of high-intensity training, thus providing a window of opportunity in which bacterial or viral illness can take hold. High-intensity training should therefore be avoided at times when an athlete has an infection or fever.

Also, high-intensity training carries with it a high risk of injury. If the athlete is ill or injured they cannot train; if they cannot train they will not improve.

Too much high-intensity training leads to overtraining. If the athlete is overtraining there will be no improvement in performance, and there may be a decrease in performance levels. If the athlete continues to overtrain, eventually they will become ill or injured, forcing them to stop.

The age of the athlete

Older athletes may not stand the physical stress of high-intensity training as well as their younger counterparts. Older athletes tend to take longer to recover from high-intensity training, are more injury prone, and heal less quickly than younger athletes. Thus it makes sense for the older athlete to spend less time at higher intensities in their training, if possible.

Children have poor local muscular endurance and limited ability to generate high-intensity anaerobic power. Because of this they do not perform well in sprints, jumps and throwing events, however they do achieve steady-state more quickly at the start of exercise, and recover more quickly following intense exercise than adults. Thus, children may need shorter resting periods than adults if performing high-intensity interval training.

The time available to train

Which sessions are carried out at high intensity and which at lower intensity is partially determined by the time available. Therefore, if on a Tuesday you only have 30 minutes

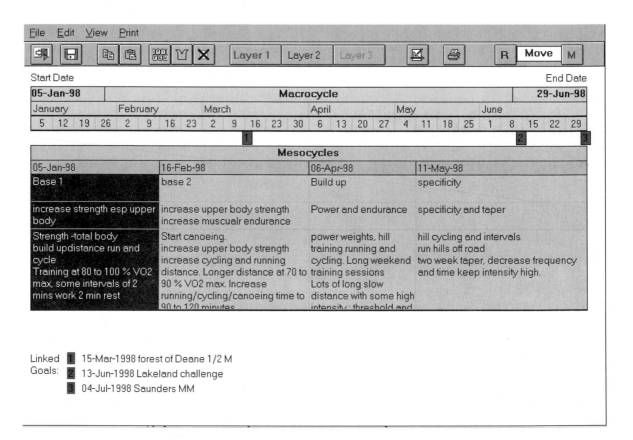

Figure 11.1 This endurance athlete has two main summer goals, three weeks apart. The first is the Lakeland Challenge, a team event involving teams of three who canoe 10 miles, cycle a hilly 26 miles over the Wrynose and Hardnott Passes in the Lake District (UK), and then run eight miles over Scafell, the highest peak in England. The second goal is the Saunders Mountain Marathon, a two-day orienteering event in which the competitors carry enough provisions for overnight camp on the hills. In this programme the athlete uses high-intensity interval training mixed with a build-up distance in the base 1 mesocycle in order to improve VO₂max. In the second mesocycle, steady-paced distance work is increased to improve oxidative ability of the muscle. During the build-up phase, threshold work is introduced and training is made more specific, on terrain similar to the race. As the races are long endurance events a long taper is needed. This athlete has planned a two-week taper

available to train, then it makes sense to do high-intensity training. This does not, however, mean that if you can only ever allow 30 minutes for training, all training should be done at high intensity. As we have seen, this is counterproductive to performance.

The season

The intensity of exercise will change depending on the season.

INTEREST

Most athletes split their training into four phases or mesocycles.

1 Conditioning – a base of skill, endurance, strength and power is formed.
2 Preparation – tends to concentrate on fine tuning skills, speed, reaction time and strategic preparation.
3 Competitive – the athlete competes.
4 Recovery – the athlete rests and recovers in readiness for the rigours of another round of training and competition.

The intensity of the exercise will differ during the different phases. During the conditioning phase intensity will tend to be lower, and during the preparation phase it will tend to be higher. Correspondingly, during the conditioning phase, volume of training will be higher, and during the preparation phase volume will tend to be lower.

♦ Cardiac drift ♦

FACT

With the onset of exercise, the heart rate increases from resting level and stabilises, usually changing very little between 5 and 10 minutes of steady state exercise. However, if exercise continues for a longer period of time, the heart rate continues to rise. This is known as **cardiac drift**, or **heart rate drift**, and is accompanied by a decrease in stroke volume.

The extent to which the heart rate drift occurs depends upon the intensity and the duration of exercise, and the training and nutritional status of the athlete. At lower intensities, the change in heart rate is less than at higher intensities; there is less heart rate drift in well trained individuals; and if the athlete remains well hydrated there is a smaller change in heart rate per given intensity of exercise.[2]

In part this increase in heart rate is thought to be caused by the increase in oxygen uptake related to substrate usage[3] (there is greater usage of fat to fuel prolonged exercise), and in part related to increases in body temperature and reduced blood volume. The reduction in stroke volume is associated with decreased venous return to the heart, due to increased peripheral vasodilatation in an attempt to promote cooling as the blood is diverted to the skin. In our attempts to promote cooling we perspire and dehydration occurs, exacerbating the reduced venous return.

When using heart rate as a measure of intensity of exercise therefore, cardio-vascular drift will affect both the safety aspects and also the training efficacy of the prescribed intensity.[4] For individuals unused to training at high intensities, using a set heart rate may add a safety feature in that, when cardiac drift occurs, maintaining the set heart rate will involve a reduction in workload. However, for individuals used to high-intensity training, using a set workload, for instance time to complete a specific distance, may be more useful when aiming for a particular training effect.

1 Coggan, A.R. and Williams, B.D. (1995) Metabolic Adaptations to Endurance Training: Substrate Metabolism During Exercise. In *Exercise Metabolism*. Ed. by Hargreaves, M. Human Kinetics
2 Montain, S.J. and Coyle, E.F. (1992) *Influence of graded dehydration on hyperthermia and cardiovascular drift during exercise.* J. Appl. Physiol. (USA) 73/4, 1340–50
3 Mole, P.A. and Coulson, R.L. (1985) *Energetics of myocardial function.* Med. Sci. Sport and Exerc. (USA) 17/5, 538–45
4 Trudeau, F., Milot, M., Pare, M. and Plourde, K. (1997) *Plasmatic response and exercise intensity adjustment in relation to heart rate and workload.* Science and Sports (France), 12/2, 123–8

Chapter 12

Intensity and Time Combine

◆ Getting the training ◆ right

A major factor in getting the training right is the combination of intensity and time.

The metabolic adaptations within skeletal muscle fibre are dependent on the combination of intensity and duration of the stimulus placed upon them. Different sports make different demands on the body, and some multi-sport athletes and team sport athletes need to train for optimum use of more than one energy system.

◆ How do I train for ◆ speed?

Sprinting relies on fast twitch fibres and on the anaerobic energy systems. Short sprint bursts, lasting less than 10 seconds, and quick bursts of maximal power such as throwing or **Olympic weight lifting**, rely heavily on the creatine-phosphate system and on the high velocity of contraction of the fast twitch fibres.

DEFINITION

Olympic weight lifting. A strength sport consisting of the combined score from two free weight lifts – the clean and jerk and the snatch.

High lactate values interfere with the creatine-phosphate system, so training for these events aims to produce maximal power without building up lactic acid, and involves maximum effort for a very short duration. Intervals of five to 15 seconds' maximum effort followed by a long recovery period of one to two minutes so that the creatine-phosphate is fully replenished and maximum effort can be repeated, produces optimum recruitment of fibres and maximum generation of force.

◆ How do I train to work ◆ for longer?

Multiple sprint sports such as football, hockey, ice hockey and basketball involve different intensities of effort at different times during the game. Some of these efforts rely on fast twitch fibres and on anaerobic glycolysis to sustain a high power output for two to three minutes. Traditionally, training for these sports includes high-intensity intervals of one to three minutes alternated with recovery periods of one to two minutes, such that lactate builds up in the muscle but a consistently high intensity is maintained throughout the training session. It is thought that this type of training trains the muscle to use glycogen in anaerobic pathways and to clear the lactate from the muscle more quickly.

The fate of lactic acid

The lactic acid is always reused as fuel. It is either turned back into pyruvate in the muscle cell or in adjacent muscle cells and used in aerobic respiration within the mitochondria, or it is cleared into the bloodstream, converted into lactate and transported to the liver where it undergoes conversion to glucose. Fast removal of lactic acid from the muscle is reflected in quick recovery from high-intensity bursts.

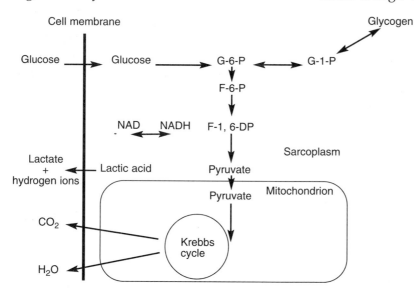

Figure 12.1 The fate of lactic acid

◆ How do I train for ◆ endurance?

For any activity that lasts longer than a few minutes, energy is supplied primarily by aerobic metabolism. For endurance-based exercise, the better you are at supplying oxygen to the muscles and the better the muscles are at utilising oxygen, the better you are able to sustain power over time. A combination of high VO_2max and ability to sustain power output close to VO_2max produces the best endurance athletes.

Increases in VO_2max

For untrained individuals there is only a small increase in stroke volume in the transition from rest to exercise. For these individuals most of the increased cardiac output needed to facilitate exercise comes from an increase in heart rate.

MAXIMUM EXERCISE			
	cardiac output	=	heart rate x stroke volume
UNTRAINED PERSON	22l	=	195bpm x 113ml
TRAINED PERSON	35l	=	195bpm x 179ml

Figure 12.2 In the trained individual, an increase in stroke volume increases the cardiac output dramatically. In fact, the highly trained endurance athlete has a cardiac output during maximum work equal to twice that of his sedentary counterpart. Generally, due to their smaller body size, women have a stroke volume of about 25% less than men and correspondingly have a lower VO_2max

Training at 60–90% of VO_2max is known to improve maximal oxygen consumption in previously untrained individuals. At intensities at or above 100%, lactic acid build-up limits the muscle cells' ability to utilise oxygen, and so the stimulus for improving maximal oxygen consumption is reduced.[1]

It is thought that training at 60–90% of VO_2max stresses the cardio-vascular system, increasing cardiac output and stroke volume and by doing so improves VO_2max. Untrained individuals may increase their VO_2max by 20% with just six months training.[2] However, in trained athletes, maximum stroke volume is reached at about 40–50% of VO_2max, thus trained individuals may have reached their genetic ceiling for VO_2max and may make no further improvements to this aspect of physiology with further training. To reach peak performance for endurance events the athlete must therefore also improve oxygen delivery to the muscles and train the metabolism such that they can sustain an intensity close to VO_2max for long periods of time.

Highly trained individuals can reach steady state exercise at greater percentages of VO_2max. That is they can work harder for longer and are more able to utilise fat at higher intensities, sparing their carbohydrate stores.

Élite cross country skiers have been recorded working at around 85% VO_2max for one hour, while well trained marathoners have been recorded training at 70–80% VO_2max for several hours.

Training increases the capillary bed in the muscle, providing a greater surface area for the diffusion of oxygen into the muscle fibres and accounting in part for the increased maximal oxygen uptake observed after training.

Training to increase the size and number of the mitochondria, the density of the capillary network and to induce the type IIA muscle fibres to work aerobically has the effect of allowing the athlete to make use of the increased oxygen delivery system and thus work at a higher percentage of VO_2max for longer. That is the athlete is able to maintain a higher intensity of exercise without significant lactic acid accumulation, or in other words have a higher anaerobic threshold. Training for these changes involves training at higher intensities – 85–100% of VO_2max for some of the time.

Learning to use fat as fuel

Competitive endurance events include those taking as little as five to six minutes to complete, and those taking several hours. Training has a different emphasis depending on where along the continuum below your sport is situated.

six minutes	five or six hours
very high intensity	low intensity
e.g. 2,000m rowing	e.g. ultra endurance running
ENDURANCE CONTINUUM	

For high-intensity, short duration endurance events such as a 2,000m rowing event, the muscles rely primarily on glycogen as fuel. As exercise is prolonged the muscle glycogen stores are used up and there is a gradual increase in the use of fat as fuel. Thus those athletes who are most able to utilise fat as fuel are better adapted to compete in long duration events.

Moderately well trained individuals can sustain exercise with an oxygen uptake of about 50% VO_2max for about an hour. Lactate accumulation, cardiac output and heart rate remain steady after about the first five minutes of exercise, that is steady state occurs. If the exercise duration is longer than this the individual becomes progressively fatigued and there is an increase in heart rate and in oxygen uptake. This increase in heart rate and oxygen uptake may be explained by the utilisation of fuels. Utilisation of fat requires more oxygen than does carbohydrate, thus the demand for oxygen increases with duration of exercise and there is a concomitant increase in heart rate for the same power output. [3, 4]

INTEREST

For a given energy yield the oxygen demand is up to 7% higher when using fat as fuel compared with using carbohydrate as fuel. As the duration of exercise increases, the contribution to energy supply from fatty acids is increased and the heart rate increases to meet the muscles' demand for extra oxygen.

The better able the muscles are to use oxygen the better able they are to oxidise fat, thus sparing the muscle glycogen stores. In fact, the ability of the muscles to use fat as fuel is directly related to the number and size of the mitochondria.

One fundamental adaptation to endurance training is an increase in the number and size of the mitochondria. This increased mitochondrial density occurs in both the slow twitch and the fast twitch fibres, providing that the intensity of exercise is great enough to recruit those fibres, and the exercise programme is maintained for long enough (in days or weeks) to allow the adaptations to remain steady. Those muscles, or fibres within the muscle, that are not recruited do not adapt. It also appears to take about four to five weeks of training for the increase in mitochondrial content to reach steady state.[5]

The magnitude of the increase in the mitochondrial density is related to both the intensity and duration of the daily training session, high-intensity or long duration sessions producing the greatest training effect.[5]

This increase in mitochondria and capillary density in the type IIA fibres increases their ability to utilise oxygen, that is to work aerobically, hence a higher intensity of exercise can be sustained without building up lactic acid, and OBLA, or the anaerobic threshold is raised.

In endurance events that rely on utilisation of fat as fuel, training at low intensities, around 50% VO_2max, for long periods of time increases the ability to mobilise and transport fat and has a psychological effect on endurance capabilities. Lactic acid accumulation interferes with the body's ability to utilise fat as fuel, thus low-intensity training promotes the ability to metabolise fat. However, given that training at intensities high enough to innervate the type IIA fibres raises the anaerobic threshold and thus reduces the lactate level for any given intensity of exercise below OBLA, this type of training also increases the body's ability to use fat as fuel. There are excellent endurance athletes who do not have startling VO_2max readings, but who can sustain intensities of 90–95% VO_2max for an hour or more. Thus different training intensities are appropriate depending on the aim of the training session and the training status of the athlete.

♦ Detraining ♦

About 50% of the increase in mitochondrial density induced through training is lost after just one week of detraining and all of the adaptation is lost after five weeks of detraining. Furthermore, to regain the adaptations lost in one week of detraining can take up to four weeks of retraining.[5]

INTEREST

- The metabolic adaptations within skeletal muscle fibre are dependent on the combination of intensity and duration of the stimulus placed upon them.
- Intervals of maximum effort of five to 15 seconds followed by a long recovery period of one to two minutes, trains the body for optimum use of creatine-phosphate, optimum recruitment of fibres and maximum generation of force.
- High-intensity intervals of one to three minutes alternated with recovery periods of one to two minutes trains the muscle to use glycogen in anaerobic pathways.
- The training emphasis for various competitive endurance events is dependent on where along the endurance continuum the event is situated.
- Endurance training increases mitochondrial density, related to the intensity and duration of the daily training session, in both slow and fast twitch fibres, high-intensity or long duration sessions producing the greatest training effect.
- This increase in mitochondria and capillary density in the type IIA fibres raises the anaerobic threshold.
- Training at low intensities for long periods of time increases the ability to mobilise and transport fat and has a psychological effect on endurance capabilities.

1 Gorostiaga, E.M., Walter, C.B., Foster, C. and Hickson, R.C. (1991) *Uniqueness of interval and continuous training at the same maintained exercise intensity*. Eur. J. Appl. Physiol. Occup. Physiol. (Germany) 63/2 (101–7)

2 Wilmore, J. and Costill, D. (1994) *Physiology of Sport and Exercise*. Human Kinetics. p. 217

3 Astrand, P.O. and Rodahl, K. *Textbook of Work Physiology* (3rd edition). McGraw Hill. p. 310

4 Kalis, J.K., Freund, B.J., Joyner, M.J., Jilka, S.M., Nittolo, J. and Wilmore, J.H. (1988) *Effect of beta-blockade on the drift in oxygen consumption during prolonged exercise*. J. Appl. Physiol. (USA) 64/2 (753–8)

5 Terjung, R.L. *Muscle adaptations to aerobic training*. GSI Sports Science Exchange #54

Chapter 13

Interval Versus Continuous Training

◆ **More than one way** ◆
to train

Every chain that breaks gives way at its weakest link. If you strengthen or replace that weak link the chain will be stronger, but somewhere there will still be a weakest link. Keep adding stress and the new weakest link will eventually break.

INTEREST

Long duration, **low-intensity** continuous exercise has been shown to improve performance in highly trained individuals. Thus élite XC skiers in Norway train at around 60% of their VO_2max for about 80% of their training time. However, huge improvements in performance times are widely documented for other élite endurance athletes in running and cycling after **high-intensity** training.

It would therefore seem that the key to improving performance lies in identifying the weakest link, creating physiological stresses that cause adaptation in that weak link, and then maintaining that adaptation while working on the next weak link. Each athlete has only one weakest link. Whether it be strength, cardiac output, ability to tolerate high levels of lactate, ability to work close to threshold for extended periods of time, or flexibility, there is always one aspect of physiology or

biomechanics that limits their performance. That weak link is individual to the athlete.

High or low intensity?

Inevitably, to stress all aspects of physiology an athlete will work at both high and low intensity at different times during their training. High-intensity work may be one continuous effort or may be as work/rest intervals.

Why do intervals help?

If we increase all elements of training at once, that is frequency, intensity and duration, we are likely to overtrain, so it is beneficial to juggle these changes. An increase in intensity is normally accompanied by a decrease in total training volume in order that the athlete does not become too fatigued.

As well as decreasing total training volume to facilitate the increase in intensity, it is often necessary to reduce the time spent at that intensity. High-intensity exercise causes acute fatigue, often due to the athlete depleting the ATP or creatine-phosphate in the muscle and to a build-up of lactic acid in the muscle. However, if the energy system that is taxed is allowed to recover the athlete may be able to repeat the effort at the same intensity, thus increasing the total volume of training time at the given high intensity.

How is it possible to work hard for longer with intervals?

High-intensity work relies more on anaerobic energy systems and thus accumulates more lactic acid.

Let us suppose that John can cycle at 15mph for a couple of hours, but at 20mph can only manage 10 minutes before he has to slow down. This is because at 20mph John starts to rely more heavily on his anaerobic metabolism and gradually accumulates lactic acid. The lactic acid blocks muscle contraction and prevents him from maintaining his pace. He feels heavy-legged and although he is trying hard he cannot maintain 20mph.

Now, if John can cycle at 20mph for just three minutes and after this time he feels fine and could continue, even though in reality his muscles are already beginning to accumulate lactic acid, his body will clear the lactic acid from his muscles if he drops his speed to 14 or 15mph for the next three minutes. He can now cycle at 20mph again for another three minutes. Working this way he may be able to achieve six or eight work intervals of three minutes at 20mph, a total of 18 or 24 minutes at 20mph as opposed to 10 minutes. Thus he has achieved a greater volume of training at a high intensity than if he tried to maintain 20mph as steady state.

Can interval training help endurance athletes?

Altering the work/rest ratio and the intensity of the work and rest intervals stresses different energy systems and recruits different fibre types.

For instance, to increase aerobic capacity by affecting central circulation:

a) you may train continuously for 20–40 minutes at around 70% VO_2max *or*

b) you may train in one-and-a-half-minute intervals at 85%–90% VO_2max with one-and-a-half-minute rest intervals.

- The first method increases heart rate and ventilation rate and for the trained individual is unlikely to cause a build-up of lactic acid.
- The second method increases the heart rate and ventilation rate, and if continued for a longer period of time would be limited by a build-up of lactic acid, but in short bursts is enough to elicit the central response while allowing enough recovery time to clear the lactate.
- The second method, however, being of higher intensity, will recruit more of the fast twitch fibres.

Which is best – interval training or continuous exercise?

This depends on the aim of the training session. To get the best from our training, sometimes we need to work at low intensities and sometimes at high intensities. When working at high intensities it is often possible to increase the overall workload, effectively working for longer at that intensity, by using interval training.

The science of interval training

A Textbook of Work Physiology by Per Olaf Astrand and Kaare Rodahl reports Dr Astrand's renowned study on the physiology of continuous exercise versus intermittent exercise or interval training. Dr Astrand studied subjects who had to achieve a given amount of work in one hour. The work was carried out either by cycling continuously at a power output of 175 watts, or in intervals with a power output of 350 watts, double the power output.

At a work load of 175 watts (with no intervals):

- the subject was able to cycle for one hour continuously
- heart rate was 134bpm
- VO_2 was 55% of maximum
- blood lactate remained near resting levels.

At a work load of 350 watts (with no intervals):

- the subject could only maintain the exercise for nine minutes
- heart rate reached 190bpm
- VO_2 was at maximum
- blood lactate had risen to 16.5 **mM**.

If the same subject cycled at 350 watts for intervals of between 30 seconds and three minutes with equal rest intervals, he could perform the desired workload within the hour.

Astrand's results clearly demonstrated that interval training allows a higher total volume of high-intensity work to be performed than continuous exercise. When working continuously the subject could work for only nine minutes at 350 watts, while when working in intervals he could continue for 30 minutes.

How long should the intervals be?

Interestingly, physiological responses differ depending on the interval duration. When the work intervals are shortened, physiological stress is reduced. In fact, even though the total work time and intensity are kept the same when the intervals are reduced, the physiological stress is much reduced as signified by VO_2, the heart rate and accumulated blood lactate shown in the table below.

The greater total volume of training at higher intensity places a greater workload on

Astrand studied the effects of continuous and intermittent high intensity exercise.[1]

Power output	Exercise condition	VO_2 l/min	Heart rate	Blood lactic acid mM
175 watts	Continuous	2.44	134	1.3
350 watts	Continuous	4.6	190	16.5
350 watts	Intermittent 30 seconds	2.90	150	2.2
350 watts	Intermittent 1 minute	2.93	167	5.0
350 watts	Intermittent 2 minutes	4.4	178	10.5
350 watts	Intermittent 3 minutes	4.6	188	13.2

* Rest duration equalled work duration in each condition.

the muscles, but the effect that it has on the heart and central circulation depends on the length of the work/rest intervals.

It is thought that during very brief intervals the build-up of lactate is reduced because the muscles utilise the oxygen that is bound to the myoglobin in the muscle cells for aerobic energy production. The recovery phase allows for the myoglobin oxygen stores to be replenished, thus the demand made on the oxygen delivery system is not severe. However, when the work interval is increased in length the myoglobin oxygen stores are depleted without subsequent replenishment during recovery periods. This results in a greater demand being made on the cardio-vascular system and in a greater build-up of lactic acid.

By shortening the work and rest periods, even to 15 seconds' work and 15 seconds' rest, it is possible to perform at very high power outputs without accumulating lactic acid or severely stressing the cardio-vascular system.[2] Thus it is possible to use interval training with short intervals, less than two minutes in length, to put an increased workload on the muscle fibres. If recruitment of fibres and demand on aerobic metabolism in the muscle cells is the aim of the session this would appear to work.

Interval training for improved central circulation

By increasing the length of the intervals to increase the demand on the oxygen delivery system, it is possible to elevate the heart rate and overload the capacity of the heart to pump blood around the body. The body's response to this is to adapt such that it increases cardiac output and stroke volume and thus pumps out more blood with each beat.

Of course, continuous training at high intensity will also have this effect, however with continuous high-intensity training a build-up of lactate causes local muscle fatigue and limits the time spent at the increased cardiac output. Interval training allows the lactate to disperse and so increases the total time spent at the increased cardiac output.

Should deconditioned individuals do interval training?

Intervals can be at any intensity, for example:

work	rest
low intensity	lower intensity

rather than

work	rest

As you can see, by varying work/rest intervals and intensity of effort, physiological stress can be reduced by working in intervals. Thus beginners to exercise can indeed get health benefits from training their heart and circulation using this method. The stress that they feel is less and so the total workload is greater if they are allowed to slow down or stop before they become too uncomfortable, and then to start again.

How do I split up the intervals?

How you split the intervals depends on what you want to achieve and what you can tolerate. Often enthusiastic sports participants try to follow the training programme of a top level athlete who is both genetically gifted and able to dedicate large portions of their life to training and resting. How much training a person can tolerate, the dosage in which they can tolerate that training and their response to that training are influenced by their genetic coding, their lifestyle, their training history and their age.

For example, working at level 4 (*see* page 17) for three-minute intervals with a three-minute rest may give one athlete just enough recovery time to be able to repeat the work interval at the same intensity for 10 repetitions. Another athlete may achieve five of the intervals, have a longer rest period, say six minutes, and then repeat the set. Each athlete achieves 10 x three-minute intervals, however one athlete achieves this in one set of 10 and the other athlete in two sets of five.

Writing a training programme is an art, directed, but not ruled, by science. Each athlete must be treated as an individual. What works for one person may not work for the next. Thus splitting the intervals up is a matter of looking at the physiological changes that you want to effect by the training, the intensity at which those intervals will be attempted, and the athlete's present capabilities. The fibre type you wish to recruit and the energy system you wish to tax will determine the work/rest periods.

Guidelines for interval times for training different energy systems

Sprint training

Short bursts of power as in sprinting and weight lifting rely on the fast twitch fibres, and the ATP supplies and creatine-phosphate systems. As lactic acid interferes with the creatine-phosphate system, the work intervals for this type of training should be short and the rest intervals long. Thus work intervals of five to 15 seconds are alternated with rest intervals of one to two minutes, such that the work time is not long enough to build up lactic acid, and a full recovery of the creatine-phosphate system is facilitated. This energy supply is sometimes termed anaerobic alactic as it is anaerobic but does not involve build-up of lactic acid.

Lactate tolerance

Work intervals of one to three minutes alternated with one- to two-minute rest intervals also stress the anaerobic energy systems. This work interval is long enough to build up lactic acid, and this type of training is called lactate tolerance. In reality, rather than training the muscles to tolerate high levels of lactate the muscles become efficient at flushing the lactate into the bloodstream. This enables the muscles to keep working at high intensities.

		Work time	Rest time
Steady state	Continuous	30–60 minutes	
Anaerobic threshold	Continuous	15–25 minutes	
Anaerobic threshold	Intervals	60–90 seconds	10–15 seconds
Lactate tolerance	Intervals	60–180 seconds	60–120 seconds
Anaerobic alactic	Intervals	5–15 seconds	60–120 seconds

Anaerobic threshold

Intervals of one minute to one-and-a-half minutes of work alternated with 10- to 15-second rest intervals raises the anaerobic threshold or point of OBLA. Continuous training at an intensity that allows you to sustain the effort for 15 to 25 minutes has the same effect. Raising the anaerobic threshold allows the athlete to sustain work at higher intensities using aerobic metabolism.

Steady state

Steady state training uses the aerobic system, and improves VO_2max and utilisation of fats.

---

1 Astrand, I., Astrand, P.O., Christensen, E.H. and Hedman, R. (1960) *Intermittent muscular work*. Acta Physiol Scand. 48:443; Astrand, I., Astrand, P.O., Christensen, E.H. and Hedman, R. (1960) *Myohemglobin as an oxygen store in man*. Acta Physiol Scand. 48:454

2 Gullstrand, L. (1996) *Physiological responses to short duration high intensity rowing*. Canadian Journal of Applied Physiology, 21(3) 197–208

Chapter 14

Strength

◆ Do I need to train ◆ for strength?

Young people generally have the strength to carry out everyday tasks, but in the elderly, even the healthy elderly, strength and power are often near to or below functionally important thresholds and they have lost the ability to perform vital tasks[1], such as getting out of a chair or climbing the stairs. Just to get dressed can result in immense fatigue, comparable to an athlete at the limit of their performance capabilities.

INTEREST

Position statements from the US Surgeon General's Office, based on world-wide research, uphold strength training as a key factor in maintaining functional ability, health and independence as we age.

Muscle strength and power decline with old age, even in completely healthy individuals. At every age the strength of a muscle is directly related to its cross sectional area, therefore age-related decline in muscle mass reduces muscle strength and power.[2]

For this reason, strength is an important part of a cross training programme, whether it be strength for health, strength to improve sport, strength to improve physique or strength to balance out aerobic work and flexibility in a general fitness programme.

◆ Women – the ◆ weaker sex?

Women are weaker than men both in absolute terms and in relation to body weight. Their poorer power–weight ratio means that they are likely to be ten years ahead of men in their increasing inability to perform daily physical tasks. This poorer power–weight ratio is reflected in the lower step heights achievable by healthy elderly women[3, 4], and in the greater prevalence of disability and falls amongst elderly women than amongst elderly men. For women involved in sports, poor strength may be reflected in increased risk of injury.

Many women are afraid to train for strength in case they build muscle, however building muscle requires a lot of dedication. Many competitive bodybuilders train for two to three hours a day for five or six days a week – their goal is not to show superior strength but to build muscle. Even given this dedication to training, in practice it is very difficult for the majority of women to build large amounts of muscle as they lack the necessary hormonal stimulus.

♦ How should I train ♦ for strength?

A strength programme should follow the principle of specificity. It should be specific to the client's immediate needs and work towards long term goals. Many variables need to be taken into account:

- which muscle groups should be included?
- should exercises be compound or isolation?
- what type of muscle action is needed (e.g. isometric, isotonic, concentric, eccentric)?

If the individual is a sports performer additional variables include:

- what are the predominant energy sources involved in the client's sport?
- are there any common injury sites involved?

If strength is to consistently increase then the programme must be progressive. It may be progressed by:

- increasing the number of reps in a set
- increasing the number of sets
- increasing the load
- changing the sets system
- changing the exercises
- increasing the number of exercises per body part.

OPINION

As with other aspects of the cross training programme, it is wise to increase only one aspect of the strength programme at a time. Generally, if the number of repetitions in a set are increased first, a subsequent increase in resistance can be accommodated by dropping the number of repetitions again.

What type of weights should I use?

Many beginners to strength work prefer fixed resistance machines to free weights, and indeed this is all that is available in some clubs and centres. Although fixed resistance machines are arguably easier to get used to, a mixture of both free weights and fixed resistance accommodates the teaching of lifting techniques that are readily transferable to everyday life, and can also, when taught well, improve body awareness and control.

When training for sports performance it should be noted that increases in strength gained from weight training may or may not translate to improved performance. Increased strength may be more applicable if resistance is added when performing the actual sport, for instance increasing the resistance on a rowing ergometer, or pushing a bigger than normal gear on a bike.

♦ Strength for sport ♦

Strength training with weights may not translate into improved sports performance. When strength training, much of the initial increase in strength comes from neurogenic changes; you learn to innervate the muscle fibres in the right sequence. Thus to be effective in improving performance, strength work needs to closely mimic the action of the sport. For this reason, when training with weights, free weights are preferable as the movement patterns are adaptable, whereas fixed resistance machines set the movement patterns for the lifter.

Working with rubber tubing or rubber bands, or working with a partner, may also provide useful resistance modes for sportspeople, however adding resistance during participation in the sport, so long as that resistance is not so great as to alter technique, may provide the most appropriate training for sports performance.

OPINION

Remember that to assist sports performance, strength training has to be specific while also maintaining body balance. The programme should take into account:

- specific muscles used in the sport either as prime movers or fixators
- joint angles
- type of contraction
- type of load
- the balance between strength and muscular endurance
- predominant energy source
- common injury sites
- previous injury sites.

Is weight training helpful to sportspeople?

This is not to say that weight training is not useful to sportspeople. Although much strength can be gained without increasing muscle mass simply by improving recruitment of fibres, strength is directly proportional to the cross sectional area of muscle. Thus if increased strength is desirable, then working towards muscle hypertrophy and at the same time working on the skill element of the sport such that you learn to utilise the increased muscle mass, may be of help.

Also, in sports that put tremendous stress on particular joint structures, increased strength built in the gym may stabilise the joint and help to prevent injury while playing sport.

INTEREST

- Increased quadriceps and hamstring strength may stabilise the knees of fell runners running down hill.
- Increased strength and muscle mass may stabilise the shoulder girdle and cervical spine of rugby players in a scrum.

Spotters

A spotter is there to help you. He/she should hand you the bar or dumbells when necessary and should stay with you to help out if you start to fail. Also he/she can take the bar or dumbells again at the end of your lift. When working with a partner you can spot for each other as well as providing encouragement for each other when the going gets tough.

When do I do my strength training?

If strength training for general fitness or health you can train all year round, however when training for sports performance the increased stress of the competitive season should be accommodated. This can be done using periodisation or cycling of training. An athlete in the competitive season needs to peak for performance and cannot put too much of their energy into a heavy weight training programme at that time. Substantial amounts of strength work can, however, be built into the off-season in preparation for competition the following year.

Order of exercises

The order of strength exercises may be governed partly by the sets system being used. For instance, a superset system requires that opposing muscle groups are worked in

	Back	Chest	Legs	Shoulders and arms	Abdominal exercises
Major muscle group exercises	• chins • lat pull-down • pullovers • single arm row • seated pulley row • deadlift (lower back)	• flat bench press • incline bench press • press ups	• deadlift • squats • lunges • step ups	• shoulder press • upright row	• abdominal curls • crunches • reverse abdominal curls • pelvic tilts • oblique curls • circle crunches
Isolation exercises	• dorsal raise • sand lizard	• dumbell flyes • pec dec	• leg extension • leg curls	• lateral raise • bicep curl • preacher curl • dumbell screw curl • tricep extension • tricep kick-back • bent over flyes	

sequence. Generally speaking it is advisable to work the largest muscle groups first using compound exercises, and the muscles of the trunk (abdominal muscles and erector spinae) last. This ensures that these important muscles are not fatigued before being used to stabilise the spine during other lifts.

How many repetitions and sets should I do?

Each time you complete a movement you have performed one repetition (rep). Put a number of repetitions together and you have a set. Strength training adaptations are slightly different depending on the load and the number of sets and reps used.

Three sets of 10 reps per exercise is commonly used, however load, number of repetitions per exercise, and rest between sets should be adjusted according to whether the emphasis is for strength or endurance. A low number of reps with a heavier load and longer rest is applicable for strength; a high number of reps with a lighter load and shorter rest period is applicable for endurance. It may be that the goal will change as the body adapts. For instance, it may be advisable to build strength first and then start to increase repetitions and reduce rest in order to add endurance.

Weight training is usually carried out in sets and reps. One rep is the performance of the lift once, a set is a predetermined number of repetitions and each set may be performed one or more times. Different combinations of sets have different terms attached to them.

How much weight should I lift?

Before you start you need to predetermine the number of reps to be used in each set and the weight that you are going to use. Once you are accustomed to lifting weights you can maximise progression by using the greatest resistance with which you can carry out the lift safely. Thus you should find your repetition maximum (RM).

Your RM is the greatest resistance that you can overcome for a particular lift. Thus the heaviest weight that can be lifted for 10 repetitions (i.e. an eleventh is not possible) is known as 10 repetitions maximum (10RM). The heaviest weight that can be lifted for six repetitions is known as 6RM, the maximum for one repetition would be 1RM.

How do I find my repetition maximum?

When beginning a weight training programme you should work well within your capabilities for each lift. However, as you progress, to get maximum benefits you will need to start overloading by using your personal RM for the number of repetitions in your set.

To find your RM decide on the number of reps needed and then load the machine (or bar) to a level that you think you can handle. Try for the number of reps you have decided on. If it was too easy you need to try again with more resistance. If you didn't complete the stated number of reps then you need to drop the resistance.

This trial and error method is hard work. Make sure that you have an experienced lifter with you to spot for you and encourage you. The spotter needs to be in a position to take the weight should you fail in your attempt to lift it. If you work out your RM for each lift in your programme all in one session you will have had a good workout. Don't attempt to then work out that day as well.

Set systems

For newcomers to weight training, each weights workout should use a whole body approach, covering all the major muscle groups and working with compound exercises, i.e. exercises that use large muscle groups and utilise more than one muscle.

Simple circuits

A useful starting point is the simple circuit. This will enable you to cover the whole body in a series of lifts and so practise your technique without overtraining. As stated earlier, newcomers to lifting should use a resistance that is within their capabilities rather than trying for repetition maximum. The simple circuit involves completing one set of each exercise performed. A programme may then read as follows.

Exercise	Reps
deadlift	10
bench press	10
lunges	10
lat pulldown	10
squats	10
alternate dumbell press	10
abdominal curls	10
dorsal raise	10

One or more circuits may be performed, depending on fitness level.

Basic sets

In the basic set each set is repeated for the desired number of times (e.g. three sets), resting for a short period in between each one.

Exercise	Reps
deadlift	10 x 3
bench press	10 x 3
lunges	10 x 3
lat pulldown	10 x 3
squats	10 x 3
alternate dumbell press	10 x 3
abdominal curls	10 x 3
dorsal raise	10 x 3

This system is used with less resistance than the RM and is therefore also suitable when working on a maintenance programme. The amount of weight used should be such that you can complete all three sets of 10, although the third set is hard work.

Delorme sets

In this system the RM is halved for the first set; for the second set three quarters of the RM is used; and for the third set the full amount is used.

If 10RM for the squat is 60kg:

First set	30kg x 10
Second set	45kg x 10
Third set	60kg x 10

Rest is allowed between each set, and failure to complete the final set may occur. Because of this it is a good idea to have a spotter on hand, especially if working with free weights.

Simple sets

In this system the RM is used for each set, and it is accepted that the lifter may fail to reach the predetermined number of repetitions towards the end of the sets. Thus the number of repetitions will automatically be reduced after the first set, despite the fact that the lifter is still aiming for the full number of reps.

If 10RM for the bench press is 40kg:

First set	40kg x 10
Second set	40kg x 8 (still aiming for 10)
Third set	40kg x 6 (still aiming for 10)

Once three sets of 10 can be performed at this weight then the resistance is increased. In this system, each set is performed to failure.

Advanced set systems

There are many other set systems, some of which were developed for strength or physique athletes which specifically aim to develop strength or physique to the limit of an individual's genetic potential. The systems outlined above are good basic lifting systems that can be used for development of muscular strength or muscular endurance.

To train for absolute strength the lifter should use high resistance and a low number of repetitions, for instance 6RM. To train for muscular endurance the lifter should use less resistance but more repetitions, up to 20RM.

1 Kernie, D.C., Dinan, S. and Young, A. Health Promotion and Physical Activity. In *Textbook of Geriatric Medicine and Gerontology* (5th edition)
2 Harridge, S.D., and Young, A. (1997) Skeletal Muscle. In *Principles and Practice of Geriatric Medicine*. Ed. by Pathy, M.S.J. John Wiley, London

3 Levi, D.I., Young, A., Skelton, D.A. and Yeo, A.L. (1994) Strength, Power and Functional Ability. In *Geriatrics*. Ed. by Passeri, M. Rome: cic Edizioni Internazioalii: 85–93

4 Young, A. (1986) *Exercise physiology in geriatric practice*. Acta Med Scand. suppl. 711: 227–32

Chapter 15

Flexibility

◆ Training for flexibility ◆

An important area of any training programme is training for flexibility. Flexibility is important for health in maintaining freedom of movement as we age, and important for sports performance in maintaining range of movement.

FACT

Flexibility is joint specific and is affected by the shape of the joint and the soft tissues around the joint and the skin. A person with great shoulder flexibility, who can easily do up a zip in the back of their clothing, may be totally unable to touch their toes without bending their knees.

The way we measure flexibility also has an effect on flexibility scores, for instance, ability to touch the toes is affected by the degree of flexion at the hip joint, the length of the hamstrings, the degree of flexion in the joints of the lower back, and indeed the size of the abdomen, or the length of the legs in comparison to that of the torso and arms.

No matter what we do to measure flexibility, ease of movement keeps us looking and feeling younger and it is possible to improve or maintain flexibility by using a full range of movement exercises and by stretching.

Should I stretch my tendons or my muscles?

Within and around muscle tissue is connective tissue – the endomysium, perimysium and the epimysium. This connective tissue is made up of elastin and collagen, the collagen being resistant to stretch. The genetically determined structure of the connective tissue, in terms of how much collagen there is in relation to how much elastin, has an effect on natural flexibility. If we are born with more collagen then we will be less flexible, more elastin makes us more flexible. When we talk about stretching we almost always talk about stretching the muscle, however, in practice, rather than the protein element of the muscle it is actually the connective tissue within the muscle belly which is resistant to stretch and which we try to affect.

Active range of movement

The active range of movement (ROM) is the range of movement possible when only the muscles affecting that movement are used. Thus to measure active flexion at the hip, a person would be asked to lift their leg up in front of them as far as possible using only their own muscle power, and the degree of hip flexion achieved simply by contracting the hip flexor muscles would be measured.

As the hip flexors are contracting to lift the leg, tension in the opposing muscle group, the hip extensors (hamstrings and gluteal muscles), causes resistance to hip flexion. The less flexible the hip extensors are, the more resistance they provide and thus the greater the strength that is required to flex the hip.

♦ Sport and flexibility ♦

DEFINITION

Muscles work in pairs. The muscle contracting to effect the movement is called the **agonist**. The opposing muscle, which has to relax in order for movement to occur, is called the **antagonist**.

Clearly then, active range of movement is affected not only by the degree of flexibility of the opposing muscle group, the antagonist muscles, but also the strength of the muscle group responsible for the movement, the agonist muscles. Active hip flexion in ballet dancers is often remarkable, demonstrating superior strength as well as superior flexibility as they lift a perfectly straight leg to shoulder height and smile sweetly.

Active range of movement is important in many sports, especially diving, gymnastics, swimming, rock climbing, sprinting, Olympic weight lifting and competitive bodybuilding.

Passive range of movement

Passive range of movement is the range of movement possible when joint movement is assisted by an outside force, as would occur if someone were to lift another person's leg up in front of them. The outside force may be another muscle group, as when we wrap a towel around the feet and pull on it with our arms in order to stretch the hamstrings, or it may be gravity, as in standing straight-legged

touching our toes, or it may be another outside influence such as another person helping us to perform stretches.

♦ Age and flexibility ♦

An inactive adult loses about five to seven pounds of muscle every decade. Therefore an inactive fifty year old has about 15–20lbs less muscle than when he/she was twenty[1], with a consequential decrease in ability to produce force. This results in the muscle groups of the lower limbs of a seventy year old being able to generate approximately 60% of the force generated by younger adults.[2, 3]

This loss of muscle mass, known as sarcopenia, can be seen as a reduction in the number of muscle fibres. Thus as we age we lose the contractile elements of the muscle and more collagen is laid down in their place. The muscles then become more resistant to stretch and we become less flexible. Added to this the opposing muscle groups lose power and exacerbate the loss of range of movement. Unless we work on flexibility and strength as we age we stiffen up.

♦ When should I stretch? ♦

Much research has been done investigating when is a good time to stretch. Most people agree that a short stretch period should be built in to the warm-up sessions performed prior to exercise to ensure that the joints have been through the full range of movement that they will be required to use during the activity.

A stretch period is also generally agreed to be useful at the end of the activity to ensure that muscles are returned to their normal resting length.

Increases in flexibility, however, are most probably more likely to occur when the muscles are not fatigued. Thus separate stretching sessions lasting between 10 minutes and half an hour may be built into the cross training programme, always remembering to stretch warm muscles. Some research shows that the more often we stretch, the more effective stretch is. Utilising a few minutes at odd times during the day to stretch can therefore be very beneficial.

♦ How should I stretch? ♦

We may improve flexibility using active or passive stretching, ballistic or static stretching, or combinations of these.

Active stretching

When we stretch using active range of movement, this is known as active stretching – we use one muscle group's contraction to put the joint through a range of movement that stretches the opposing muscle group. Sitting or standing upright and pulling the shoulder blades together by contracting the muscles of the upper back stretches the muscles of the chest. This is an active stretch.

Ballistic stretching

Often this type of stretching involves bouncing at the end of the range of movement. Kicking the legs up in the air in front of you as in the Can-Can is a ballistic stretch. Straight-legged toe touching, bouncing downwards towards the floor is a ballistic stretch. While undoubtedly effective in improving flexibility, ballistic stretching carries with it a high risk of damage to the muscle or joint.

Active stretching without ballistic movement is, however, a very effective way of simultaneously increasing flexibility and strength specific to active ROM.

Passive stretching

Passive stretching involves an outside influence moving the limb and so taking the joint through to the end of its range of movement. Sitting on the floor with a towel or belt around your feet and pulling the body forwards towards the thighs stretches the hamstrings and lower back passively. Lying on your back on the floor while a partner lifts your straight leg up into the air and through to the end of your range of flexion is also passive stretching. This does not involve strength from the opposing muscle group.

Static stretching

Static stretching occurs when the joint is moved slowly towards the end of its range of movement and is held still. This type of stretching carries with it less risk of injury than does ballistic stretching.

♦ Stretch reflex ♦

When a muscle is stretched, nerve receptors situated in the muscle cells set off a nervous reflex causing that same muscle to contract and oppose the stretch. The faster the stretch movement, the stronger the contraction will be. This is known as the stretch reflex or myotatic reflex and acts as a safety mechanism. As the joint moves towards the end of its range of movement the risk of injury to joint structures and soft tissues increases, thus in order to prevent this the muscle contracts and moves the joint back towards the neutral position.

If, when stretching, we move slowly into the stretch until we feel resistance from the muscle, and at that point hold the position still, i.e. static stretch, the stretch reflex will be overcome and the muscle will again relax, allowing us to move slowly further into the stretch.

Golgi tendon organ reflex

Golgi tendon organs (GTOs) are nerve receptors located within the tendons. Putting tension on a tendon as may occur during a stretch, but more often occurs during a muscle contraction, may fire the golgi tendon organ reflex causing the muscle to relax. The GTOs sense that the tendon is under tension and therefore in a precarious position, and when they fire they set off a reflex relaxation in the muscle in order to release tension on the tendon.

This particular reflex facilitates the more advanced method of stretching called peripheral neuromuscular facilitation.

Peripheral neuromuscular facilitation (PNF)

PNF stretching utilises the GTO reflex by purposely putting the tendon under tension, thus causing the reflex action of muscle relaxation.

To use PNF stretching you move slowly into the stretch position until you feel the muscle is under stretch, wait for the stretch reflex to be overcome and at that point move further into the stretch position until the muscle is under tension. Holding this position, contract the muscle hard isometrically, that is contract or tense the muscle without any movement

occurring at the joints and hold this contraction for six to 10 seconds.[4] This will put tension on the tendons and fire the GTOs. Now relax the muscle and wait for a few seconds for the muscle to relax, allowing you to move slowly further into the stretch.

CRAC

CRAC stretching is a combination of active stretching with PNF stretching. Muscles work in pairs, an agonist and an antagonist As one muscle contracts, its antagonist relaxes to allow movement around a joint to occur. This is known as reciprocal innervation.

FACT

CRAC stands for:
 	
       Contract
       Relax
       Active
       Contract.

To use CRAC follow the PNF method of stretching. Move slowly into the stretch position, waiting for the stretch reflex to be overcome in the antagonist. Contract the muscle hard isometrically for six to 10 seconds. Then Relax the muscle and wait for a few seconds. Actively Contract the agonist to move slowly further into the stretch.

As you actively contract the agonist, reciprocal innervation will cause the antagonist to relax even further.

To stretch the hamstrings by this method:

- lie on your back on the floor and raise one straight leg, leaving the other leg bent at the knee with the foot flat on the ground
- holding the back of the raised leg with your hands or a towel, move slowly to stretch the hamstrings and wait for the muscle to relax
- now contract the hamstrings hard for six to 10 seconds by pushing the leg down towards the ground, against the towel, but do not let the leg move
- relax the muscle
- contract the hip flexors to move the leg towards your chest and further into the stretch.

1 Evans, W. and Rosenburg, I. (1992) *Biomarkers*. New York, Simon and Schuster
2 Young, A. (1992) Strength and Power. In *Oxford Textbook of Geriatric Medicine*. Ed. by Evans, J.G. and Williams, T.F. Oxford University Press, pp 597–601
3 Davies, C.T.M., Thomas, D.O. and White, M.J. (1986) *Mechanical properties of young and elderly human muscle*. Acta Med Scand suppl 711: 219–26
4 Hardy, I. (1985) *Improving active range of hip flexion*. Res. Q. Exerc. Sport. (USA), 56/2 (111–14)

This method of stretching is very effective in increasing active range of movement as it simultaneously stretches one muscle while strengthening the opposite muscle.

◆ Is stretching ever ◆ bad for me?

If you have lax ligaments around a joint you may have a hypermobile joint. In this case strengthening the muscles to stabilise the joint and protect it from injury is more appropriate than stretching these muscles.

Muscles that are sore from being overworked should not be stretched until the soreness dissipates.

Chapter 16

Warm-up and Cool-down

♦ Warm-up ♦

When chemicals are mixed together in a test tube a reaction will occur more easily if the test tube is warmed. The body is similar. Generally it works better after a warm-up.

Increasing efficiency and reducing the risk of injury

During exercise the muscles demand an increase in the blood supply. This is partially met by greater cardiac output due to an increase in heart rate, and partially by redirection of blood to the working muscles.

Like the test tube experiment, the chemical reactions taking place in the body during exercise are speeded up if the body is warm. Muscle and connective tissue making up tendons and ligaments become increasingly pliable when warm, and finally a warm-up facilitates the response of nervous tissue, thus activating fibres transmit impulses more quickly and feedback is more efficient.

These acute changes during warm-up for exercise increase the body's efficiency and reduce the chance of injury from inaccurate movement patterns, from tearing or straining cold muscles, or from spraining joint structures.

Reducing build-up of lactic acid

At the start of exercise the sudden increase in demand for energy from the working muscles is met largely by the short term anaerobic supplies which are quick to respond. As exercise continues the contribution from the aerobic system gradually increases, characterised by an increase in both respiration rate and heart rate.

At the onset of exercise, because the sudden increase in energy supply is largely dependent on the anaerobic systems, there is an increase in lactic acid production within the cells. Gradually the amount of energy supplied by the aerobic system increases to a point where it is able to meet the energy demand, and the accumulated lactic acid is turned back into pyruvate and utilised as fuel. Steady state is reached.

INTEREST

If the energy demand at the onset of exercise is high, then large amounts of lactic acid build up in the cell and the anaerobic threshold is soon reached. Steady state may still occur, but with a higher residual level of lactic acid present. The residual level of lactic acid in the muscles may be close to threshold level. In this case even a slight rise in intensity of exercise, as may happen when running up a small hill, is likely to increase muscle lactate beyond threshold level, forcing the athlete to slow down.

A gradual and progressive warm-up may prevent this situation by allowing muscle lactate to clear so that a lower residual level is set when steady state is reached. After steady state is achieved, this will allow for small rises in intensity, without crossing the anaerobic threshold.

Optimising energy supply from fatty acids

Lactic acid inhibits the utilisation of fat as fuel, forcing the muscle to use vital glycogen stores. Thus high residual levels of muscle lactate effectively drain the muscle glycogen stores, decreasing the ability to sustain long duration exercise. Gradual progressive warm-up therefore allows for optimum usage of fat as fuel and optimum glycogen sparing.

What is the best way to warm up?

The warm-up is preparation for exercise. Warming up should involve a gradual increase in the intensity of exercise, utilising the muscles that will be used during the sport, and a gradual increase in the range of movement around the joints used in the sport. Clearly in some sports such as cycling or resistance training on machines, the movement patterns are very regular, while in other sports such as fell running or training with free weights they are far less so. Some sports, for instance gymnastics, require extreme ranges of movement. During the warm-up, range of movement should gradually increase to mimic that used during the activity.

Once the muscles are warm a short period of stretching facilitates joint range and muscle lengthening. The intensity of exercise should then be gradually increased again until steady state is reached.

♦ Cool-down ♦

Cool-down might better be termed reparation. The cool-down period exists to gradually disperse lactic acid from the muscles and to return contracted muscles to their resting state.

If lactic acid has built up in the muscle cells it will be more quickly dispersed if we continue to exercise at a reduced rate, thus allowing aerobic metabolism to use up some of the lactic acid, and pumping blood through the muscles dispersing the remainder more quickly.

Post-exercise stretching (cool-down stretch)

Some activities, such as gymnastics or some dance or martial arts training, may in themselves utilise full range of movement, however, other activities use restricted ranges of movement. If the joints are never moved through their full range of movement then reduced flexibility will ensue. Thus a programme of stretching is advisable as part of any training programme. As muscle is more pliable when warm, this is the time that it should be stretched, therefore it is customary to stretch post-activity while the muscle is warm and while we are still in training clothes that do not in themselves restrict range of movement.

This post-exercise stretch, sometimes termed cool-down stretch, in no way precludes the addition of specific stretching sessions to a programme. It simply ensures that after restricted range of movement activities we return the muscle to its resting length, and offers a convenient time to perform exercises aimed purely at increasing flexibility and range of motion.

♦ When is a cool-down not ♦ a cool-down?

We should be warm to stretch. Thus after stop-and-go activities such as weight training it may be more appropriate to stretch the relevant body parts straight after each exercise, or to use a cardio-vascular activity to warm up again in order that the muscles are warm enough to stretch after the training session.

Similarly, when standing in the freezing cold after a race, stretching should be kept to a minimum, if done at all. In this instance we should at least put warm clothing on before we stretch, and should probably go home, have a warm bath and then stretch.

Post-exercise stiffness

There is much discussion on post-exercise stiffness. The fatigue that occurs directly at the end of strenuous exercise is most probably due to low glycogen stores, fatigued nerve pathways and a build up of lactic acid. The lactic acid will disperse fairly quickly once exercise ceases, though restoring glycogen stores may take one or two days, depending on nutrition.

The soreness that occurs in muscles one or two days after an exercise session is delayed onset muscle soreness (DOMS). This is most probably due to a number of factors, including micro trauma in the muscle cells and leakage of enzymes that then irritate the nerve endings. Depending on severity this trauma may take a few days to heal and the soreness may take a few days to be relieved. Severe DOMS is a sign that the training session was too much for the training status of the athlete.

Cross training and DOMS

When suffering from DOMS the sore muscles should be rested. Thus cross training accommodates recovery without loss of fitness by offering alternate training which stresses different muscle fibres. DOMS is a symptom of muscle damage and injured muscles need to rest and heal.

Putting it All Together

Chapter 17

Programme Structure

♦ Programme structure ♦

Among all the variable factors associated with cross training one thing is certain. To be completely successful, a cross training programme has to be structured.

OPINION

A haphazard approach to cross training will at best give haphazard results, and at worst will increase the risk of injury. The success of cross training is bound up in the skill, expertise and knowledge of the programme designer. Understanding the principles of cross training will assist the trainer in designing programmes that maximise the benefits while minimising the risks.

There are many ways to write a training programme. It is estimated that without a structured programme an athlete will reach only 75% of their potential. A haphazard approach to training may predispose an athlete to injury from overtraining by overdeveloping some muscles and underdeveloping others, or by inadequately preparing the athlete for the physiological stress of competition.

QUOTE

'Genotype is also strongly involved in determining the response to regular exercise and to an increase in fitness.'
CLAUDE BOUCHARD[1]

Each person is a unique individual and each of us responds to training in a different way, thus we each need an individual training programme. Following someone else's programme may provide us with guidelines, but fails to take into account each individual's particular circumstances, unique history, unique genetic ability and response to training.

◆ Writing a cross training ◆ programme

If we were to play God to the world, we would firstly look at the whole to decide what we wanted for the future of the world. Then we would need to examine each nation, how they interacted and whether they were progressing in a way that would enhance their own future and that of the world. Occasionally we would need to look at the whole again so as to make sure that it was still moving in the right direction.

To write a cross training programme we must play God to the body. We must look at the whole multi-faceted picture and determine exactly what we want from the programme. Then we must examine all the individual pieces and make sure that each individual piece is set up right. Periodically we must look at the whole picture and make sure that it still all fits together well.

◆ Programming for ◆ health/fitness

When putting together a cross training programme for general health and fitness purposes, rather than for any specific competitive achievement, the immediate issue is which activities you like to do. A mixture of activities that cover strength, endurance and flexibility for both upper and lower body will give an all-round fitness base.

Thus when choosing training modes you should look at a balance of these three areas of fitness. For example, swimming provides endurance and flexibility training, so adding a strength-based activity such as a strength circuit will provide the balance. Tai chi provides flexibility and strength training, so adding a cardio-vascular activity such as

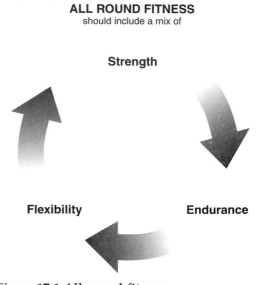

ALL ROUND FITNESS
should include a mix of

Strength

Flexibility   **Endurance**

Figure 17.1 All-round fitness

walking will provide balance. Having decided on the training modes, then training frequency, intensity and time can be manipulated to ensure a safe and effective programme.

How often, how hard, and how much for health/fitness?

The ACSM guidelines suggest that for health purposes, aerobic exercise of a moderate intensity should be undertaken for 30 minutes most days of the week. For fitness purposes, aerobic exercise of a vigorous intensity should be undertaken for 20 minutes three times per week, and two strength training sessions each incorporating one to two sets of eight to 10 exercises (eight to 10 repetitions of each) covering most of the body should be undertaken each week.

How this is incorporated in a cross training programme for health then depends on the circumstances, likes and dislikes of the individual.

- How often can you realistically make time to train?
- For how long can you train at each session?
- What do you like to do?

Take the following examples.

1 John works all week and spends time with his family at weekends. He knows that every evening he can spend a total of one hour and 35 minutes training. This allows him 20 minutes' travelling time from work to the gym, 30 minutes' training time, 15 minutes' showering time, and 30 minutes' travelling time from the gym to home. This means he is home around 7.30p.m. which is just tolerable for his family. Weekends are strictly family time.

John likes to train with weights and on cardio-vascular machines, except steppers, and he also likes to cycle. He sets up his training programme to allow him three gym-based sessions of 30 minutes and two cycle sessions.

On Tuesdays and Thursdays he goes straight home from work and then goes out cycling from home. This allows him an extra 20 minutes as he has cut out the travelling time to the gym, so he cycles for 50 minutes to an hour.

On Mondays, Wednesdays and Fridays he goes home via the gym. Mondays and Wednesdays he does a strength-based circuit on resistance machines. On Fridays he joins in a circuit class that mixes aerobic work and strength/endurance work. The class is an hour long, so if he and his wife have anything planned for Friday night he may miss it.

Thus most weeks John follows the ACSM guidelines and does a total of three aerobic sessions at least 20 minutes in length, and achieves two strength-based sessions. He also performs stretches at home later in the evenings.

2 Frances is at college. Her timetable allows the odd free afternoon or morning. She works three evenings a week in a restaurant and has varying degrees of studying to complete in her own time. For her, scheduling regular day by day activity is difficult to say the least. She cannot afford to join a gym and in any case dislikes training in fitness studios or gyms.

Frances sets up her programme by attending one dance class on Wednesday afternoons. As she is studying drama this fits in nicely with her studies, and also achieves one session of mixed activity with flexibility worked in. It is difficult to categorise this session as it is sometimes aerobic and sometimes anaerobic, so she counts it as muscular endurance and flexibility.

Timetable for John (1)

Day	Activity	Duration
Monday	Strength-based resistance machines plus flexibility	30 minutes
Tuesday	Cycle plus flexibility	50–60 minutes
Wednesday	Strength-based resistance machines plus flexibility	30 minutes
Thursday	Cycle plus flexibility	50–60 minutes
Friday	Circuit class aerobic and muscular endurance	60 minutes

Timetable for Frances (2)

Day	Activity	Duration
Monday	Run	30 minutes
Tuesday	Walk	30 minutes
Wednesday	Dance plus muscular endurance and flexibility	90 minutes
Thursday	Walk	30 minutes
Friday	Circuit class aerobic and muscular endurance	60 minutes
Saturday	Run	30 minutes
Sunday	Water circuit plus strength and endurance	60 minutes

Two days a week Frances runs for 30 minutes. Every day of the week she walks to and from college. This involves 15 minutes brisk walking, adding up to half an hour every day. On most Sundays she attends a water circuit class which involves a mix of strength and endurance work.

Frances also meets the ACSM minimum guidelines for health through dance and circuit training, running and walking, and is most of the way to achieving their minimum guidelines for fitness.

The body only adapts to unaccustomed stress

For both John and Frances, once their body has adapted to their training such that it is no longer difficult, they will plateau at that fitness level. The body only adapts to unaccustomed stress. If they have no wish to improve further that is fine, they are meeting the guidelines for fitness and health. However, if they want to improve further in any aspect they will have to change something, e.g. frequency, intensity, time or type of exercise. Without a goal it is difficult to decide what to change. It may be that change

is forced upon them; a new instructor may start to take the class and change the intensity of the training, or the length of the class; Frances may move further from college and must now walk for twenty-five minutes each way, changing the duration of her training sessions; John may buy a mountain bike and start to ride off-road as well as on-road, automatically adding more upper body work to his programme.

Currently, John is pleased with his improvements in fitness and decides to enter a 100-mile sponsored bike ride to raise money for a local charity. He now has a specific achievement goal. He has become a sportsperson and will have to plan his programme even more specifically if he is to be successful.

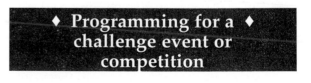

♦ Programming for a ♦ challenge event or competition

If the cross training programme is leading to a challenge, event or a competition, then the programming has to be more focused and a more scientific approach is valuable.

Training pyramid

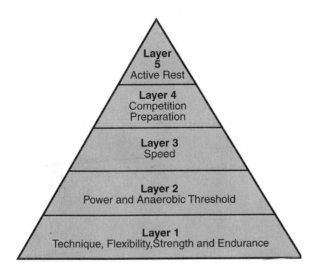

Figure 17.2 Training pyramid

Many aspects of training need a firm base from which to build. For instance, power is a combination of strength and speed but power training subjects the body to extreme forces and must therefore be done from a firm foundation of strength, both to facilitate the power and to protect the musculo-skeletal system from injury.

The first priority, therefore, in building a training programme is to build a firm base from which refinements such as speed, power and reaction time may be added. Finally, event or competition preparation may include tapering, psychological preparation, nutritional preparation, etc.

Periodisation

Training can be systematically split into training phases or layers. While there may be considerable overlap from one phase into another, splitting training up in this way allows the athlete to focus on one or two limiting factors, thus maximising the efficiency of their training time.

As explained in chapter 7, the whole training programme that leads up to an event is called a macrocycle. Chunking down the training period or macrocycle into phases allows for focusing on the weak links. These training phases are called mesocycles.

A break from tradition

Traditionally competitive sports split the training macrocycle into four mesocycles.

1 Conditioning.
2 Preparation.
3 Competition.
4 Recovery.

In reality the number of mesocycles included is less relevant than the concept of this system and the end result for the athlete. Thus the structure that I have laid out below breaks from tradition and splits the macrocycle into five phases. I have included two conditioning phases as mesocycle one and mesocycle two, which allows for separate training aims such as strength and power to be delineated.

Mesocycle one
The first mesocycle occurs out of season and is used to ensure adequate skill, flexibility, endurance and strength to support the rest of the training and competition. This mesocycle should be used to focus on technique, to improve flexibility, to build endurance, to rehabilitate from any injury and to correct

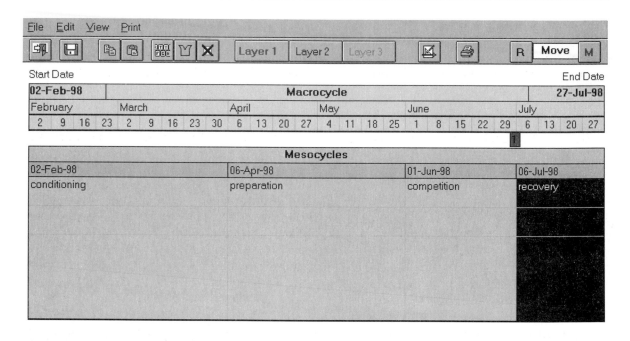

Figure 17.3 The four competitive sport mesocycles. These do not have to be of equal length in time

muscular imbalances that may predispose towards injury. Thus for a marathon runner this mesocycle may include a considerable amount of lower body flexibility and strength work, while for a canoeist the emphasis will be on upper body work and on technique.

For sports involving power, where increased muscle mass may be of benefit, muscle hypertrophy utilising high-volume, high-intensity weight training may come into this mesocycle. One of my clients whose sport was hangliding and who was naturally of light build, spent this mesocycle building muscle so that he had the weight to control his glider.

Cross training is an ideal tool to use in mesocycle one. Improvements to central circulation are training specific rather than sport specific, thus changes to the heart and central circulation occur whether we run or cycle for example.

Likewise, cross training using weight training, circuit training or other forms of resistive work may be used to increase strength.

> **OPINION**
>
> Tai Chi may increase strength and balance for climbing, while ballet may improve flexibility, grace and presentation skills for posing in bodybuilding.

Mesocycle two

Mesocycle two is used to build on endurance or power. Thus the endurance athlete would increase mileage to ensure that they could cope with the racing mileage, while a marathon runner would build up to just below marathon distance and a 10km runner may build up to overdistance, such that running 10km felt easy.

During this mesocycle an ice hockey player may concentrate on increased power, and towards the end of this mesocycle and the beginning of the next on being able to recover from and repeat that power output.

In sports where power output is important, plyometric training, jumping, bounding and leaping may be included during this mesocycle. This phase should therefore become more specifically related to the sport, however cross training may still prove useful. For example, a distance runner who was previously plagued by injuries when embarking on high-mileage training may still include a fair amount of cycling or in-line skating. This would enable them to increase the volume of endurance training without greatly increasing the amount of impact on the joints.

Equally, this athlete may continue with strength training, though at a reduced volume, in order to minimise muscular imbalance and maintain muscle strength, thus stabilising joints that were previously prone to injury. Flexibility work in the form of dance or martial arts may also be continued.

Finally during this phase the power athlete may reduce the volume of strength training, utilising lower reps and sets, but increasing load and speed of movement and shifting towards more sport specific and multi-joint exercises such as bench press, deadlift and lunges.

Mesocycle three
During mesocycle three, specd, agility and reaction time are built into the programme.

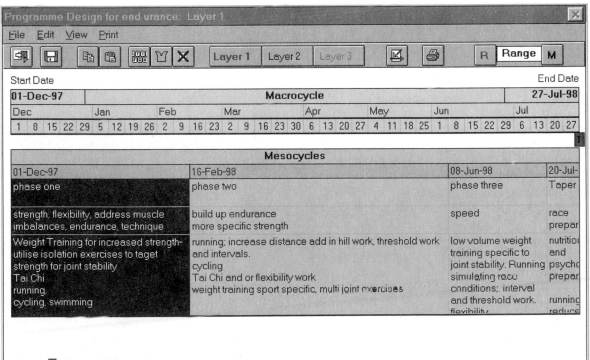

Figure 17.4 Example of an endurance athlete's phased programme utilising cross training

Also during this mesocycle, skill work and drills for team sports are practised. The endurance athlete will build up to work at race pace and conditions and may compete in time trials and minor races; fell runners and mountain marathoners would spend much training time on the hills, if possible on terrain similar to that on which they will race; mountain bikers will attempt to simulate race conditions; multiple sprint athletes will work on speed, repeatable power and bursts of speed, agility reaction time and skill. Where matches/events are part of extended tournaments these conditions should also be simulated.

Strength athletes such as powerlifters would become very sport specific in this mesocycle, decreasing the volume and in-creasing the intensity of work, and simulating competition by attempting one repetition maximum lifts, while bodybuilders would be reducing fat levels and practising posing routines. Where possible training time should match the time of day of the competition.

For single sport athletes cross training should be much reduced in this mesocycle, as at this stage sport specific training is vital to achieving the best performance.

Mesocycle four
Mesocycle four is the taper for the event. The length of the taper is dependent on the scale of the event; a long taper is required for distance athletes, a shorter taper for sprint

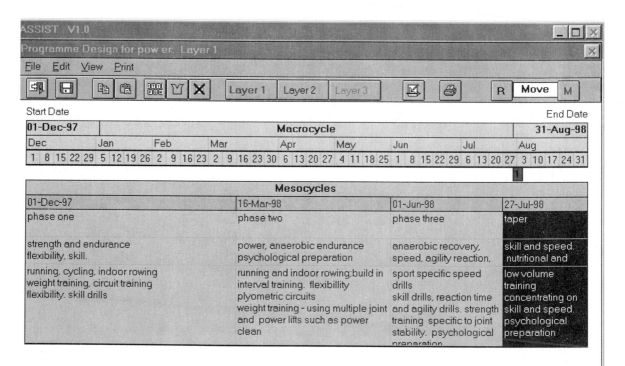

Figure 17.5 Example of a multi-sport athlete's phased programme utilising cross training

athletes. During the taper there is a decrease in volume of training while the intensity remains high. Changes to psychological and nutritional preparation may accompany this.

In sports where there is a competitive season this mesocycle may include the main part of that season, during which the aim is to maintain or improve performance levels.

Mesocycle five

Mesocycle five is a rest mesocycle. Active rest should be maintained for one to four weeks before the whole process starts again in preparation for the next season. Cross training is very appropriate to this mesocycle, training being low volume, low intensity and low pressure/stress.

Microcycles

Having divided the training into mesocycles, each one progressing a particular part of the training, then each week's training can be planned. The mesocycles can be split into smaller sections. These are called microcycles and are very often, though not always, one week long.

Mesocycles				
04-Aug-97	03-Nov-97	16-Feb-98	25-May-98	31-Aug-98
kayak	base 1	base 2	speed	competition

Microcycles				
04-Aug-97 (13 weeks)		kayak		
learn to kayak		skill training - kayak strength and enurance aimed specifically at kayak navigation improve body composition		
04-Aug-97	11-Aug-97	18-Aug-97	25-Aug-97	01-Sep-97
7 days	7 days	7 days	7 days	7 days
cycle 1 runx3 weightsx2 kayak x1 rowx3	cycle 1 runx3 weightsx3 kayak x1 rowx3	cycle2 runx3 weightsx3 kayak x1 rowx3	cycle2 runx4 weightsx3 kayak x1 rowx3	cycle 2 runx4 weightsx3 kayak x1 rowx3

Figure 17.6 The mesocycles are split into microcycles and the training level can be progressed from one microcycle to the next, planning how many sessions of each discipline should be included

Daily plans

Current Microcycle Details:	cycle 1 runx3 weightsx2 kayak x1 rowx3			

Date	Type of Exercise	Intensity	Time/Dur	Notes
10-Aug Sun				
11-Aug Mon				
12-Aug Tue	run/row			1 hour very easy- easy row 20 min
13-Aug Wed	weights			5 sets to failure upper body
14-Aug Thu	kayak			2 hours steady
15-Aug Fri	run			30 mins easy
16-Aug Sat	run			1.5 hours run
17-Aug Sun				
18-Aug Mon	run/row			30 mins, row 3,500 17.12.4
19-Aug Tue	weights			5 sets to failure
20-Aug Wed	cycle/swim			
21-Aug Thu	kayak			
22-Aug Fri				
23-Aug Sat				
24-Aug Sun	run			9 miles ish- hilly
25-Aug Mon				
26-Aug Tue	run/row			45 minsrun;1/1mininte intsX5X2 row
27-Aug Wed	weights/run			5 sets to failure

Figure 17.7 Once each microcycle or each week of training is planned, the training can be planned on a daily basis

Individual sessions

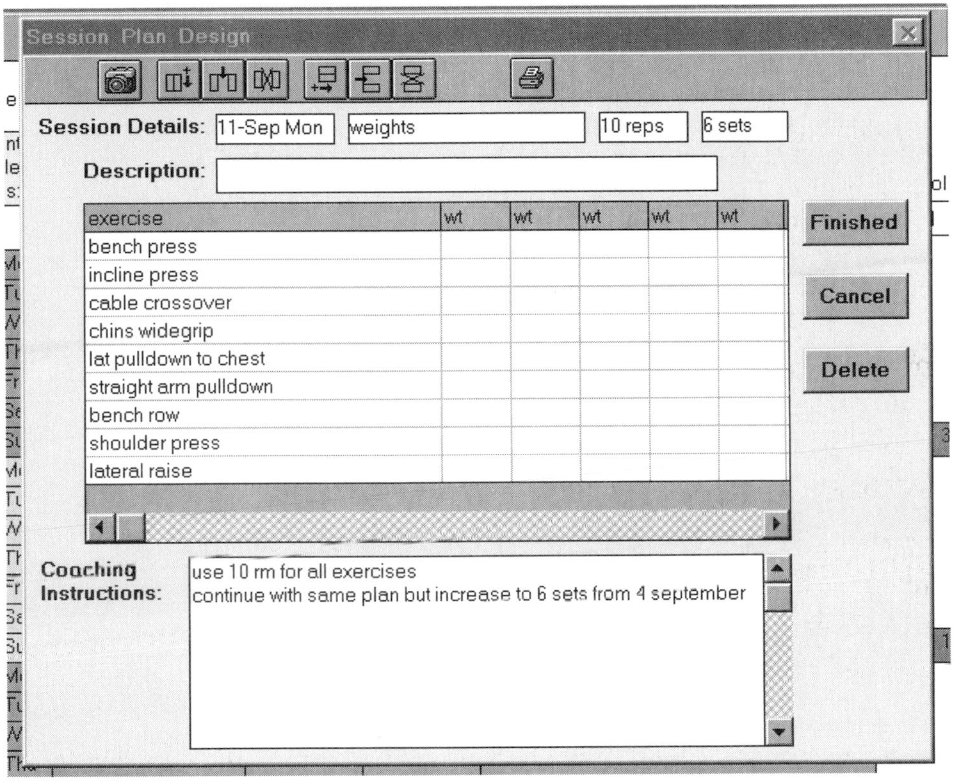

Session Plan Design

Session Details: | 11-Sep Mon | weights | 10 reps | 6 sets

Description:

exercise	wt	wt	wt	wt	wt
bench press					
incline press					
cable crossover					
chins widegrip					
lat pulldown to chest					
straight arm pulldown					
bench row					
shoulder press					
lateral raise					

Finished

Cancel

Delete

Coaching Instructions: use 10 rm for all exercises
continue with same plan but increase to 6 sets from 4 september

Figure 17.8 Finally, individual sessions can be planned on each day

115

Why do some athletes change their training at different times of the year?

As you can see from the training mesocycles it is possible to alter the training focus at different times of the year in order to achieve improved performance. Many athletes simply add in extra work, assuming that more is better. This is not the case. In fact, to benefit from increased intensity in training it is often necessary to reduce the total training volume. Increasing the intensity increases the stress on the body, thus necessitating increased recovery time if we are to benefit. Reducing training volume can be achieved by reducing either frequency or time or a combination of both.

Thus, at different times of the year, when the athlete is in different periods or mesocycles of training, both the volume and intensity of training will change.

Training load

Overall training load is often used as a measurement and can be manipulated in such a way that when volume of training is high, intensity is low, and vice versa. Training load is often measured by combining intensity and volume. For example, a runner may measure intensity by perceived exertion rated between 1 and 5, and volume by time in minutes. In one week he may run for five days in total (**programme one**), and out of that five days he does one long slow run, two runs at a steady pace, one threshold run and one interval session of five three-minute intervals.

Programme One						
Day	Time in mins	Reps	Total time	Intensity	Load	Load, running total
Monday	40	1	40	2	80	80
Tuesday	3	5	15	4	60	140
Thursday	60	1	60	2	120	260
Friday	90	1	90	1	90	350
Sunday	20	1	20	3	60	410
					Total load 410	

Load is calculated by multiplying time by intensity

The next week he may run for six days in total. He may do one long slow run, three runs at a steady pace, one threshold run and one interval session of six three-minute intervals (**programme two**).

Programme Two						
Day	Time in mins	Reps	Total time	Intensity	Load	Load, running total
Monday	40	1	40	2	80	80
Tuesday	3	6	18	4	72	152
Thursday	60	1	60	2	120	272
Friday	90	1	90	1	90	362
Saturday	60	1	60	2	120	482
Sunday	20	1	20	3	60	542
					Total load 542	

The total training load has increased by 132 from week one to week two. In this instance the training load is not a specific measure but is simply an estimation of by how much the training load is increasing or decreasing. Thus if in week two the two steady runs became a swim and a run and the long run became a cycle but the intensity and time remained the same, then the total training load would be the same (**programme three**). Of course, the physiological stress may be less as the cross training would reduce some of the repetition and joint impact problems that can occur with single sport training such as running.

Programme Three						
Day	Mode and time in mins	Reps	Total time	Intensity	Load	Load, running total
Monday	run 40	1	40	2	80	80
Tuesday	run 3	6	18	4	72	152
Thursday	swim 60	1	60	2	120	272
Friday	cycle 90	1	90	1	90	362
Saturday	run 60	1	60	2	120	482
Sunday	run 20	1	20	3	60	542
					Total load 542	

By watching the training load it is possible to make sure that the programming is progressing at a reasonable rate, with no sudden large jumps in volume or intensity, and also that easier recovery weeks and tapers are built into the programme.

For weight training, repetitions and sets may be used to calculate the training load.

Day	Mode	Reps	Sets	Load	Load, running total
Monday	weights	10	3	30	30
Wednesday	weights	10	3	30	60
Friday	weights	10	3	30	90
				Total load	90

Load is calculated by multiplying reps by sets

Or the calculation method may be more sophisticated and utilise total repetitions and resistance, in which case the loads would have to be calculated per lift and then added together.

Day	Lift	Reps	Sets	Total reps	Resistance	Load	Load, running total
Monday	deadlift	10	3	30	70kg	2100	2100
Wednesday	deadlift	10	3	30	70kg	2100	4200
Friday	deadlift	10	3	30	75kg	2250	6450
Monday	bench press	10	3	30	50kg	1500	7950
Wednesday	bench press	10	3	30	55kg	1650	9600
Friday	bench press	10	3	30	55kg	1650	11250
						Total load	11250

As you see, the more complex the system, the more accurate the tracking of load becomes. However, a simple tracking of load estimation may be enough to ensure that training is progressing in the right direction, either increasing in total or tapering, and may flag up any sudden increases or drops such that they can be examined for validity before the athlete embarks upon the training.

| 🖫 | ✄ 🖻 🖹 | 🎛 | Layer 1 | Layer 2 | **Layer 3** | | 🖨 |

Training Session Plan for Mesocycle: Start Date: **03-Mar-97**

Current steady run x3 interval run LSD x 1 bike 20 miles, swim 30 mins
Microcycle
   Details:

Volume of:

All ▼

Date	Type of Exercise	Intensity	Time/Dur	Notes
> 07-Mar Fri	rest day			
08-Mar Sat	run	1-2	15 miles	easy
09-Mar Sun	bike	2	20 miles	steady
10-Mar Mon	run	2-3	12 miles	steady - somewhat hard
11-Mar Tue	run	3	6 reps	intervals
12-Mar Wed	run	2	14 miles	steady
13-Mar Thu	swim		30 mins	
14-Mar Fri	rest day			
15-Mar Sat	run	2	17 miles	easy
16-Mar Sun	bike	2	20 miles	steady
17-Mar Mon	run	2-3	6 miles	steady - somewhat hard
18-Mar Tue	run	3	8 reps	intervals
19-Mar Wed	run	1-2	17 miles	steady
20-Mar Thu	bike	2	20 miles	steady
21-Mar Fri	swim		30 mins	
22-Mar Sat	rest day			
23-Mar Sun	run	2-3	13 miles	half marathon RACE Fleet
24-Mar Mon	swim		30 mins	

117

144

119

Figure 17.9 In this programme the 'volume of' column on the far right conveys total load for each week. It is calculated by multiplying intensity and time for each session and adding them together through the week. Thus the load initially increases from 117 to 144 and then during the week of the half marathon drops to 119

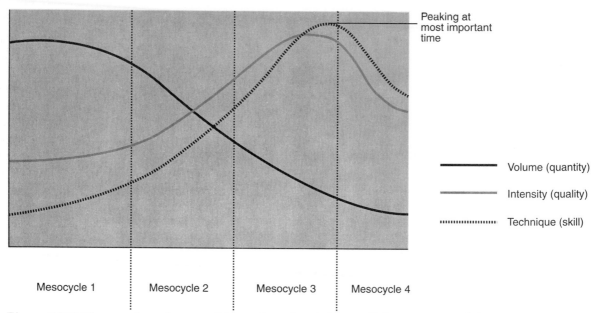

Figure 17.10 Changes in volume and intensity of training at different times of the year (hypothetical)

In figure 17.10 the hypothetical training year culminates in a competitive period when the intensity of training is at its peak and the volume of training is low. Immediately after the competition mesocycle the intensity of training drops, however volume is also relatively low at this point as active recovery takes place. The increase in volume that follows would be shadowed by increases in intensity until volume drops once again to allow for high-intensity training.

♦ There is more than one ♦ way to skin a cat

It is possible to elicit the same physiological response by more than one method of training. For example, training to raise anaerobic threshold can involve one continuous training session or interval training.

OPINION

Many people believe that to lose body fat you must work aerobically and at low intensities. In fact, losing body fat is a matter of creating a calorie deficit. It is a case of calories consumed versus calories expended. To lose body fat you must expend more calories than you consume. How you do that is largely irrelevant. Thus you can work at high intensity for half an hour or at low intensity for one-and-a-half hours – as long as the calorific requirement is the same, the choice is yours. You can choose to mix weight training with cardio-vascular training or you can choose to add in high-intensity aerobic work or even plyometrics or sprinting. Again, the choice is yours.

Similarly, in bodybuilding circles many people advocate a preferred method of training in order to gain maximum size or increased definition. Proponents of every

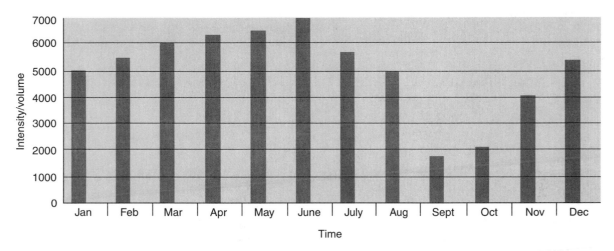

Figure 17.11 In this example load gradually increases and then drops in July and August during competition. September brings a recovery phase and then the load starts to rise again

method can quote many examples of success as evidence that their favourite method works best.

A look at the imbalance of musculature between the dominant arm and non-dominant arm in a tennis player, or the dominant leg and non-dominant leg in a squash player; or a look at the muscular back of a rower, or the legs of a speed skater will show that heavy resistance training is not the only way to increase muscle bulk.

In summary, each individual is different and the training methods chosen rely on variations of FITTA (*see* page 59) and are dependent on physiological response, determined by assessing the limiting factor of a person's performance and that person's individual response to training.

1 Bouchard, C. Discussion: Hereditary Fitness and Health. In *Print Exercise Fitness and Health. A Consensus of Current Knowledge.* Ed. by Bouchard et al, Human Kinetics, Illinois

Chapter 18

Programmes for Different Types of Athlete

♦ The single sport ♦ athlete

OPINION

Research clearly shows that for single sport athletes nearing their genetic ceiling for performance, cross training is not the best way to achieve the tiny increments in performance that make the difference between winning or losing. For sports performers, cross training programmes that are designed without regard for the primary sport may actually increase the incidence of injury.[1] Indeed, even in untrained individuals, the aerobic benefits from a single sport are the same as those from cross training given similar volume and intensity of training.[2]

Single sport athletes need to determine why they are cross training, and then vary the training depending on the mesocycle they are currently working in. For these athletes cross training may not be appropriate all year round.

It may be that they cross train during active rest. 'Cross train to work your body while resting your mind' (Dr Stephen Seiler); it may be that they cross train only during the off-season to build on base line fitness parameters such as flexibility, aerobic power or strength, or to alter muscular imbalances that negatively affect technique in their sport, but should then focus on the individual sport as the competitive season gets

QUOTE

'The National Collegiate Athletic Association (NCAA) has gathered statistics over a three-year period in the early '90s showing that women suffered anterior cruciate ligament injuries more often than men, nearly four times as often in basketball, three times as often in gymnastics, and nearly two-and-a-half times as often in soccer . . .

. . . Many factors have been discussed as the source of women's tendency to tear their ACL more often. Some are based on anatomical realities such as a narrower femoral notch, increased Q angle, increased ligamentous laxity, inadequate strength, and impaired neuromuscular co-ordination . . .

. . . Strength training for women is critical, with an emphasis on being in shape before they play their sport. Women tend to be generally more flexible than men, but a programme that consists of strengthening and stretching is essential for all athletes involved in sport. Non-competitive balance and agility training may enhance proprioceptive function and help to reduce the rate of injury as well.'

NISMAT website, Hot Topics page on *Knee Injuries and the Female Athlete*, http://www.nismat.org/hot

closer. It may be that they cross train when rehabilitating from injury in order to maintain high levels of fitness without aggravating the injury; or it may be that they cross train throughout the season to correct or maintain muscular balance and avoid recurrence of injury.

Whatever the reason for cross training, the single sport athlete must keep their primary goal in mind.

Case study

One of my clients who lived in London was a mountain marathoner. His sport included orienteering competitions run over two days somewhere in the mountains of the United Kingdom or Europe. He typically travelled 25–30km over rough, hilly country with few, if any, footpaths on each day of competition. Often the weather was stormy, and throughout the competition he carried provisions for the two days and for an overnight camp on the hills.

As he lived in central London, sport specific training, i.e. running on the hills with a pack, was only possible when he could get a couple of day trips to the hills, so much of his training had to be a compromise. At one time he plodded the streets of London with a pack, however he found that London streets were too busy to allow him to keep moving, and the extra weight of his pack increased the impact on his joints which, when pavement plodding, predisposed him to knee injury. He tried running on a treadmill at an incline with his pack which was an improvement, but he got very hot running indoors and also he found it slightly embarrassing to run in a club with a pack on his back. Finally he decided to seek help.

We structured his training programme to include weight training to build upper body strength so that he suffered less upper body fatigue during the event. We also included lower body work with free weights (deadlift, squats and lunges) so that he had the strength to keep his joints in alignment during both uphill and downhill running over rough country.

INTEREST

Note that downhill running works the eccentric contraction of the leg muscles, especially the quadriceps (thighs), thus by strengthening this phase using the downward motion involved in squats and lunges, eccentric strength is trained. This will benefit the athlete in stabilising the knee joint during downhill running. Free weights are better than fixed resistance in this instance as they also use other fixator muscles, simulating fixation when running with a pack.

The weight training improved and maintained strength enough to allow him to reduce the amount of time he spent running with a pack, and he no longer ran with a pack when running on pavements or on the treadmill. We added intervals and hill work on the treadmill, and circuit training which added agility and power work to his training. This was to help with balance on the rough ground and his ability to descend quickly, and he started to cycle to and from work for extra endurance training without extra impact on the joints. At weekends he travelled out of London into Epping Forest or on to the North Downs (about one hour's travel time each way) as often as possible and this provided some rougher country to train on. Nearer to the time of his events he increased his trips to the hills for specific training. On his weekend trips he ran with a pack.

He found that because he was undertaking a greater variety of training he did not get stale but trained more and harder, so not only

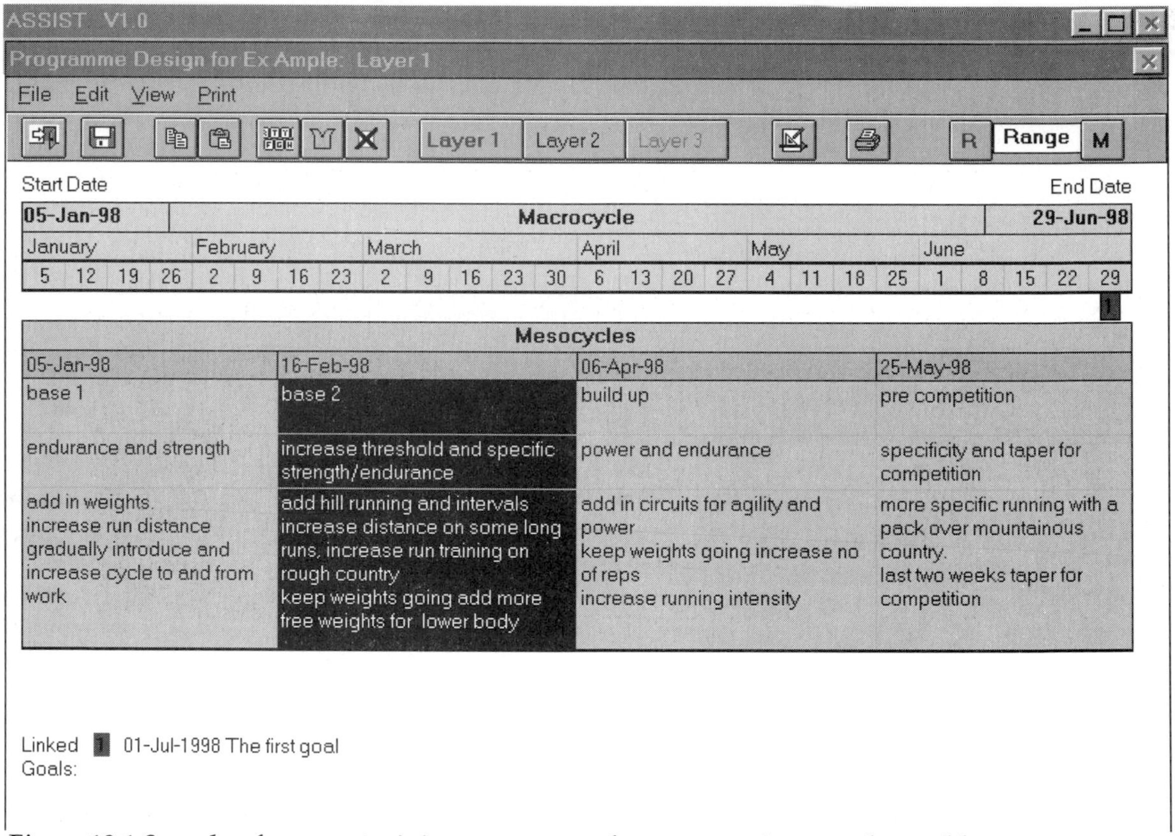

Figure 18.1 Sample of a cross training programme for a mountain marathon athlete

did his performance in mountain marathon improve, but also because of the variety and the improvement in his fitness levels he found it easier to motivate himself to train.

For the single sport athlete, cross training activities aimed at the same physiological changes may improve performance depending on the activity involved. For example, UK sports coach and sports physiologist, Tony Lycholat, noticed that runners who took up road cycling during rehabilitation from injury reported improvements in performance, whereas runners who used a rowing ergometer during rehabilitation suffered deteriorating performance levels.

He surmised that the reason for this was that the speed of joint movement, utilisation of energy systems, and velocity of contraction of fibres in spinning the pedals on a bike, caused similar physiological stress to performance running, whereas the slow cadence of row training, normally less than 30 strokes per minute, placed different physiological stress on the body and therefore elicited a different adaptive response.

It would seem sensible then that a single sport athlete looking to use cross training as part of their training programme should choose disciplines that closely mimic fibre type recruitment, energy system utilisation and speed of movement of their primary sport.

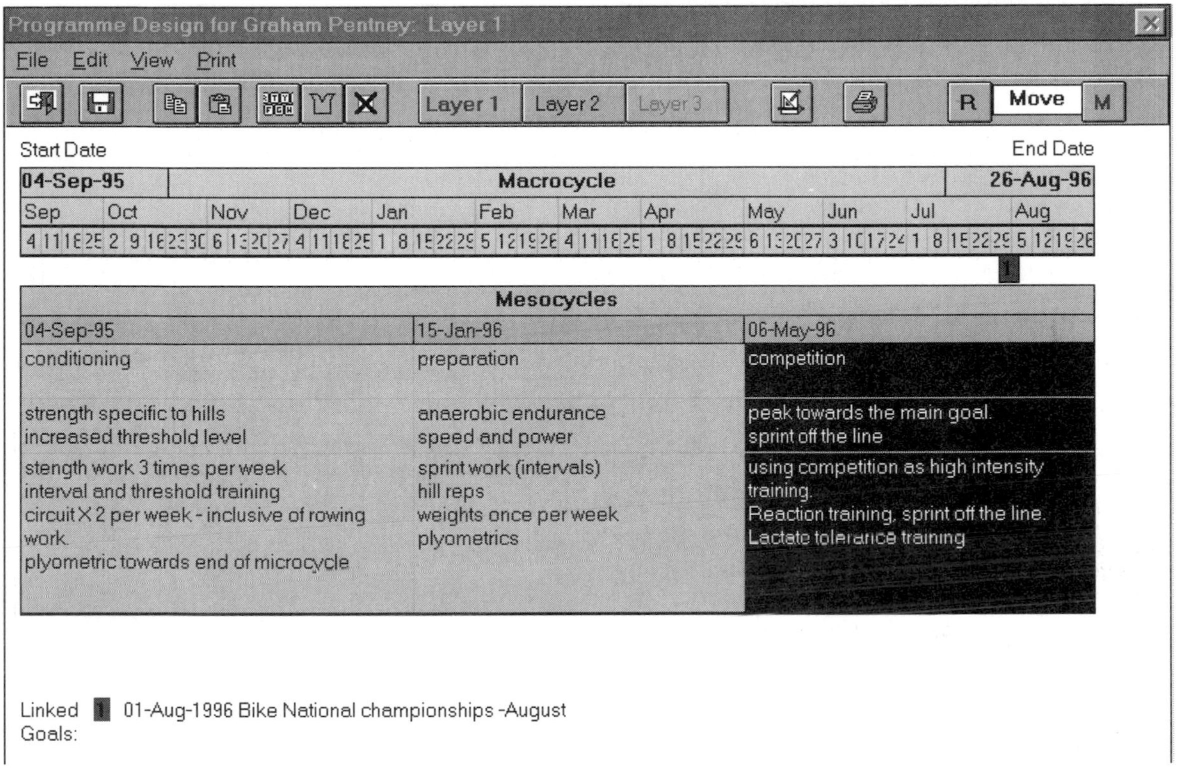

Figure 18.2 This mountain biker cross trains using circuit training, weight training and indoor rowing in his conditioning mesocycle. He drops the rowing in his preparation mesocycle, and has a long competitive mesocycle in which he only cycles. In this phase he does low- and moderate-intensity cycling during training sessions, and uses races as high-intensity training sessions. He will, however, taper for the national championships in August and following them have a recovery phase

Notwithstanding this, many single sport athletes may have other, perfectly sound, reasons for cross training using non-compatible disciplines. If strength of the athlete is the weak link in performance then that athlete may well choose weight training; if reaction time is the weak link the athlete may play table tennis.

OPINION

Train according to the needs of the individual athlete. Each athlete has one weak link that prevents them from improving. Train to strengthen the weak link and then look for the next weak link.

◆ The recreational ◆ athlete

For recreational athletes the same applies. They may cross train to alter muscle imbalances, to recover from injury or simply as a change from single sport activity. If they cross train they may become more enthusiastic about training because of the variety, they may then train more and improve in their sport simply because the volume of training is higher.

Cross training plan for a recreational marathon runner

Week	Mon	Tues	Wed	Thurs	Fri	Sat	Sun	Total run
1	X20	5S	X20	6S	R	8S	11S	30
2	3F	4S	X25	8S	5F	R	13S	33
3	X25	3F	X30	6F	6F	R	15S	30
4	X35	6S	X40	8S	6F	R	15S	35
5	X40	5S	X45	3F	5F	R	17S	30
6	X50	8S	X55	5F	X55	R	20S	33
7	X60	3F	4F	10S	X60	R	18S	35
8	3F	3S	R	3F	R	R	Marathon	35

R = Rest day – make sure you stretch.
X = Cross train, e.g. swim or cycle. Number denotes time in minutes.
F = Fast run. Number denotes mileage.
S = Slow run. Number denotes mileage.

🖫	✂ 📋 📋	⬚	Layer 1	Layer 2	Layer 3		🖨	

Training Session Plan for Mesocycle: Start Date: **23-Feb-98**

Current Microcycle Details:

Volume of:

[All ▼]

Date	Type of Exercise	Intensity	Time/Dur	Notes
23-Feb Mon	run	2	3 miles	steady
24-Feb Tue	run	3	3 reps	intervals
25-Feb Wed	run	2	5 miles	steady
26-Feb Thu	swim		30 mins	
27-Feb Fri	rest day			
28-Feb Sat	run	1-2	12 miles	easy pace
01-Mar Sun	bike	1-2	20miles	steady
02-Mar Mon	run	2	6 miles	steady
03-Mar Tue	run	3	4 reps	intervals
04-Mar Wed	bike	2	20miles	steady
05-Mar Thu	run	1-2	12 miles	easy pace
06-Mar Fri	swim		30 mins	
07-Mar Sat	rest day			
08-Mar Sun	run	3	6 miles	10K RACE
09-Mar Mon	run	1	4 miles	easy pace
10-Mar Tue	run	3	5 reps	intervals
11-Mar Wed	bike		15miles	
12-Mar Thu	run	2	8 miles	steady

(57)

> (94)

Figure 18.3 Section of a cross training plan for a recreational runner using cycling and swimming

♦ The fitness athlete ♦

With the widespread popularity of health clubs and gyms containing both cardio-vascular and weights equipment, a new breed of sportsperson has emerged. These people often present the trainer with a significant challenge in that they want to achieve apparently totally incompatible goals, for example: 'I want to build muscle and run a marathon.'

To accommodate the competitive nature of this new breed of sportsperson, gym-based X-training challenges such as the ultrafit challenge and TV-based Gladiators have grown up.

These challenges are generally a mixture of strength and endurance, speed and agility. They demand that the trainer use imagination and ingenuity linked with a sound understanding of physiology in order to write a training programme that will assist the fitness athlete in achieving the desired results.

Sometimes these multi-sport athletes simply have a number of different sports that they are keen to compete in. The competitions may be in different disciplines but they are each separate events, for example the athlete whose training programme is detailed in figure 18.6, on page 130, competes in 10km and half marathon road races, mountain marathons, indoor rowing competitions, mountain biking, and gym-based challenges, as well as completing non-competitive ultra distance outdoor challenges.

127

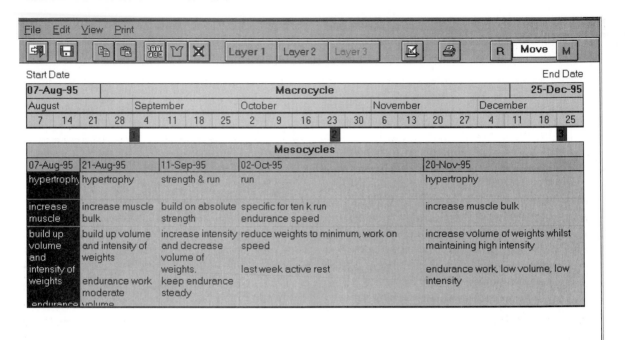

File Edit View Print

Layer 1   Layer 2   Layer 3   R Move M

Start Date   End Date

| 07-Aug-95 | Macrocycle | 25-Dec-95 |

Start Date / End Date
07-Aug-95 Macrocycle 25-Dec-95

August	September	October	November	December
7 14 21 28	4 11 18 25	2 9 16 23 30	6 13 20 27	4 11 18 25

Mesocycles

07-Aug-95	21-Aug-95	11-Sep-95	02-Oct-95	20-Nov-95
hypertrophy	hypertrophy	strength & run	run	hypertrophy
increase muscle	increase muscle bulk	build on absolute strength	specific for ten k run endurance speed	increase muscle bulk
build up volume and intensity of weights	build up volume and intensity of weights	increase intensity and decrease volume of weights.	reduce weights to minimum, work on speed	increase volume of weights whilst maintaining high intensity
endurance	endurance work moderate volume	keep endurance steady	last week active rest	endurance work, low volume, low intensity

Linked   ▪ 03-Sep-1995 triathlon
Goals: ▪ 26-Oct-1995 10 Kilometre run
         ▪ 25-Dec-1995 build bulk

Figure 18.4 This fitness athlete wanted to build muscle, however he also wanted to compete in a triathlon and a 10km run. Thus rather than follow the traditional mesocycle phasing his programme is aimed at building bulk, with phases of increased endurance training designed to complete his endurance goals without losing too much of his hard-earned muscle

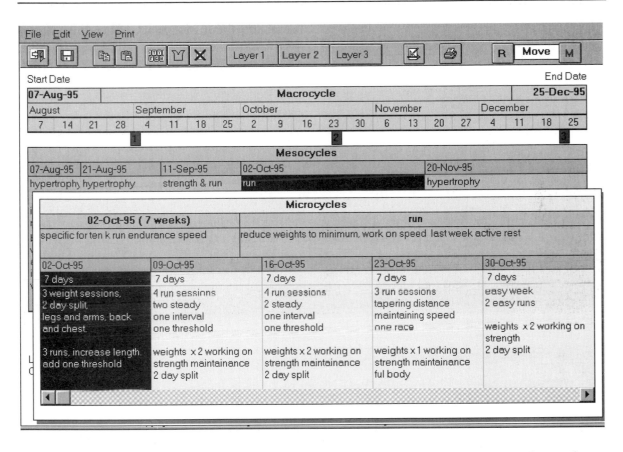

Figure 18.5 The programme outlined in figure 18.4 has now been broken down into microcycles

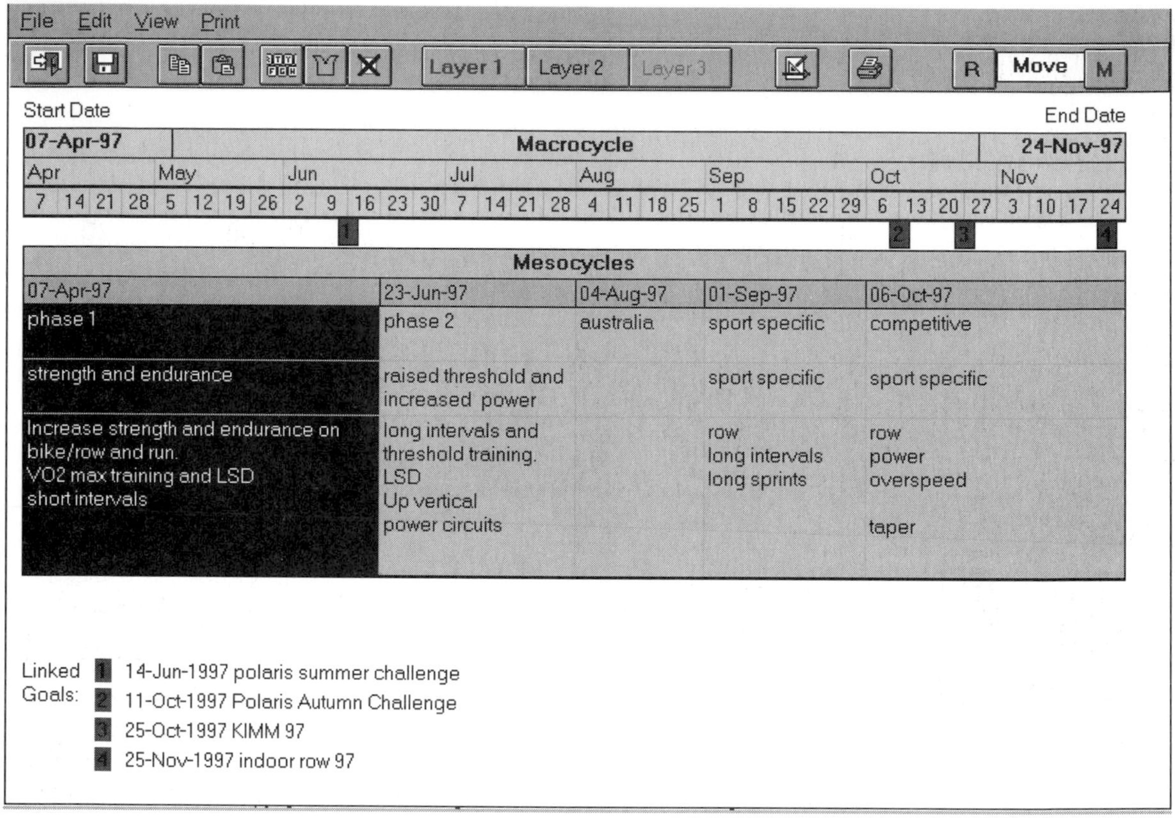

File	Edit	View	Print

| | | | | | | | Layer 1 | Layer 2 | Layer 3 | | | | R | Move | M |

Start Date   End Date

07-Apr-97	Macrocycle	24-Nov-97

Apr	May	Jun	Jul	Aug	Sep	Oct	Nov
7 14 21 28	5 12 19 26	2 9 16 23 30	7 14 21 28	4 11 18 25	1 8 15 22 29	6 13 20 27	3 10 17 24

Mesocycles

07-Apr-97	23-Jun-97	04-Aug-97	01-Sep-97	06-Oct-97
phase 1	phase 2	australia	sport specific	competitive
strength and endurance	raised threshold and increased power		sport specific	sport specific
Increase strength and endurance on bike/row and run. VO2 max training and LSD short intervals	long intervals and threshold training. LSD Up vertical power circuits		row long intervals long sprints	row power overspeed taper

Linked   **1**   14-Jun-1997 polaris summer challenge
Goals: **2**   11-Oct-1997 Polaris Autumn Challenge
         3   25-Oct-1997 KIMM 97
         4   25-Nov-1997 indoor row 97

Figure 18.6 In this macrocycle the athlete has two mountain bike challenges, a mountain marathon and an indoor rowing championship. In the middle of the macrocycle he has planned a month's trip to Australia during which he will be scuba diving

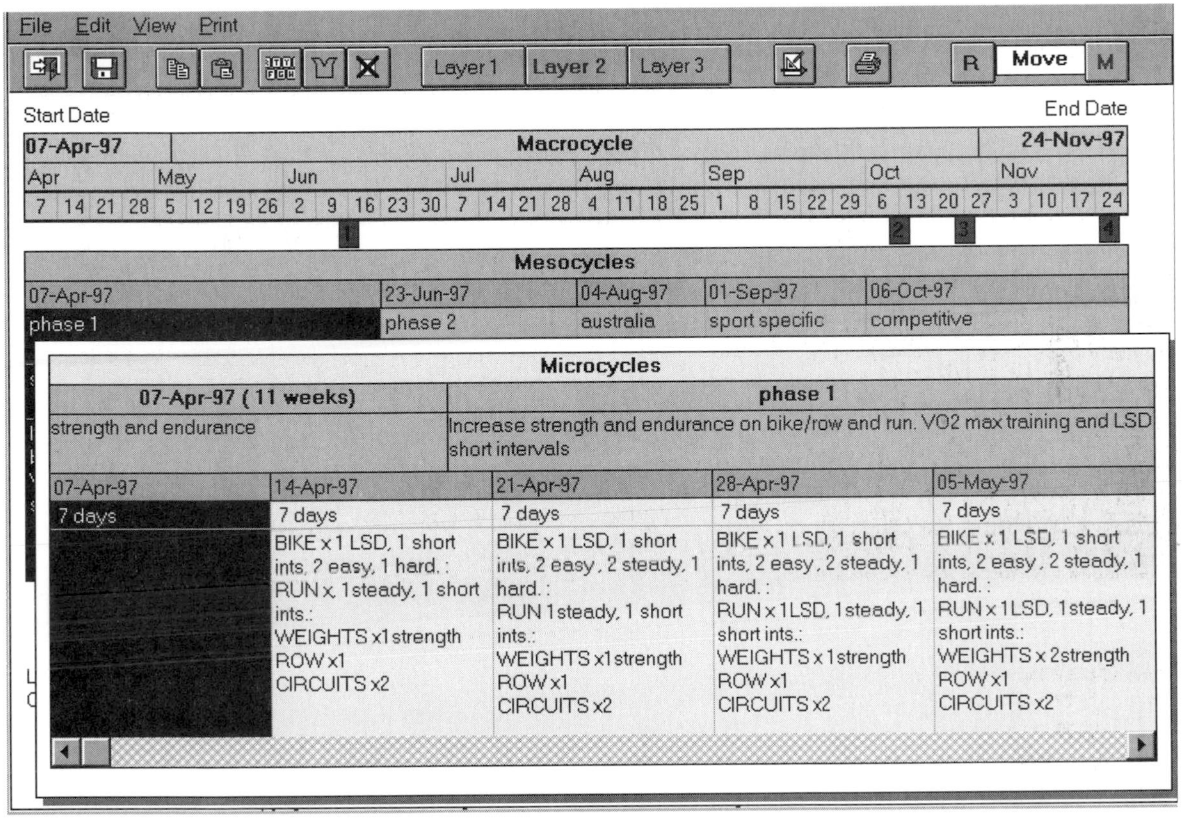

Figure 18.7 The athlete has five mesocycles, the first concentrating on strength and endurance. Towards the end of this first mesocycle is his first major challenge, a two-day mountain bike competition

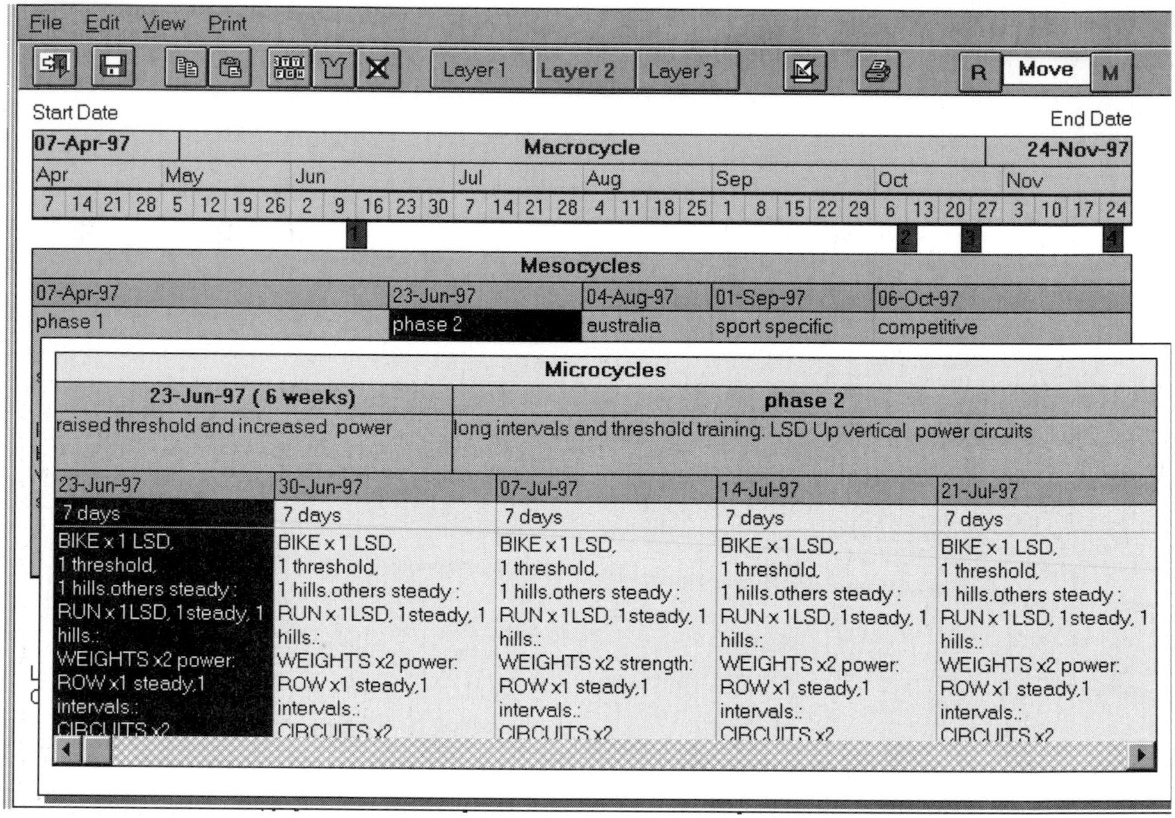

Figure 18.8 In the second mesocycle the athlete concentrates on increasing power and anaerobic threshold. During his trip to Australia he will attempt to keep up enough short duration, high-intensity training to maintain these adaptations

| File | Edit | View | Print | | | | | | | | | | | | | | |

| | | | | | | Layer 1 | Layer 2 | Layer 3 | | | | | R | **Move** | M |

| Start Date | | | | | | | | | | | | | | | | End Date |

| **07-Apr-97** | | | | | | | | | Macrocycle | | | | | | | **24-Nov-97** |

| Apr | | | | May | | | | Jun | | | | Jul | | | | Aug | | | | Sep | | | | Oct | | | | Nov | | | |
| 7 | 14 | 21 | 28 | 5 | 12 | 19 | 26 | 2 | 9 | 16 | 23 | 30 | 7 | 14 | 21 | 28 | 4 | 11 | 18 | 25 | 1 | 8 | 15 | 22 | 29 | 6 | 13 | 20 | 27 | 3 | 10 | 17 | 24 |

Mesocycles

07-Apr-97		23-Jun-97	04-Aug-97	01-Sep-97	06-Oct-97
phase 1		phase 2	australia	sport specific	competitive

Microcycles

06-Oct-97 (8 weeks)		competitive		
sport specific		row power overspeed taper		

27-Oct-97	03-Nov-97	10-Nov-97	17-Nov-97	24-Nov-97
7 days	7 days	7 days	7 days	7 days
BIKE x1 hills, 1 intervals: RUN x1 steady: WEIGHTS x1 power ROW x1 power, 1 overspeed, 1 time trial, 1 short ints. CIRCUITS x2	RUN, 1 steady: ROW x2 threshold 3000:1x 1500 ints: 1x1000 ints.. CIRCUITS x2	ROW x2 threshold 3000:1x 1500 ints: 1x1000 ints.. CIRCUITS x2	ROW x2 threshold 3000:1x 1500 ints: 1x1000 ints.. CIRCUITS x1	Taper ROW1x 1500 ints: 2x1000 ints, INDOOR ROW CHAMPIONSHIPS

Figure 18.9 During his last mesocycle the athlete has one major mountain bike competition. Again this is a two-day event and is followed just two weeks later by a mountain marathon, also a two-day event. In the final few weeks of this mesocycle he cuts right back on cross training in an attempt to peak for the British Indoor Rowing Championships, in which he took 51st place completing 2,000m in six minutes, 28.6 seconds

♦ The multi-sport ♦ athlete

Multi-sports are by definition competitive cross training events.

Heptathlon

- 100m hurdles
- High jump
- Shot put
- 200m sprint
- Long jump
- Javelin
- 800m

Decathlon

- 100m sprint
- Long jump
- Shot put
- High jump
- 400m sprint
- 110m hurdles
- Discus
- Pole vault
- Javelin
- 1,500m

The modern, or military, pentathlon is based on the skills needed by a battlefield courier and was first included in the Olympic Games of 1912. From 1952 to 1992 it was a team event. Modern pentathlon is a five-day contest involving five events:

- an equestrian steeplechase over a distance of about 450m
- a series of épée fencing matches
- pistol shooting at standing silhouette targets
- a 300m freestyle swim
- a 4,000m cross country run.

Scoring is on a point basis, the individual and team winners being decided by total scores from the five events.

However, as for single sport events the athlete must focus on the needs of the sport. Often multi-discipline events such as pentathlon, heptathlon or decathlon require considerable skill in a number of the disciplines, for example javelin throwing, jumping events and hurdling in the heptathlon and decathlon. In addition to the technique training involved, different types of fitness are required for different events as well as the mental toughness to train for all of these events. This often means that the athlete must spend most of their training time on improving their least favourite discipline. Multi-sport athletes who combine events in this way are remarkable and dedicated athletes.

In contrast, triathlon and modern pentathlon are multi-sport events. Traditionally encompassing swim, road bike and road run, triathlons now often include mountain bike, a cross country or fell run and rowing or kayaking. Similarly, and growing from the challenge of triathlon, there is a huge increase in the popularity of adventure sports.

Adventure racing is set to return to New Zealand in November with the announcement today that Wanaka is to be the opening venue for this years Southern Traverse.

As in previous years the location of the race course is still kept a secret until the night before the race, but in the announcement today the organisers confirmed that there will be three mountain passes, two paddling sections, three mountain biking sections, and a huge (175m + 75m) abseiling section.

The race is due to start on Monday 10th November and it is expected that the first competitors will reach the finish line in Queenstown after 4 days and some 350km of racing.

TAKEN FROM SOUTHERN TRAVERSE MEDIA RELEASE, 22ND OCTOBER 1997

Multi-sport for the adventurer includes events such as rock climbing, horse riding, cycling or mountain biking, fell running, kayaking or canoeing and mountaineering. Most often they are team events, the whole team having to complete the whole course. This tests both the skill and fitness of the individuals in the team and the ability of the team to work together.

Training for multi-sport challenges

For the multi-sport athlete the challenge is to combine skill and fitness training to meet the demands of all the disciplines or events involved in the sport. Cross training must be used wisely in order to get maximum benefits.

To write a cross training programme for multi-discipline sports a long term approach must be taken. Firstly, the top priority event must be identified. For instance a triathlete who is pretty reasonable at swimming, cycling and running, may make cycling his top priority as this is the furthest distance with the potential to make up the most time. However, for someone who is a poor swimmer, swimming may become priority as they may be losing too much time on this event.

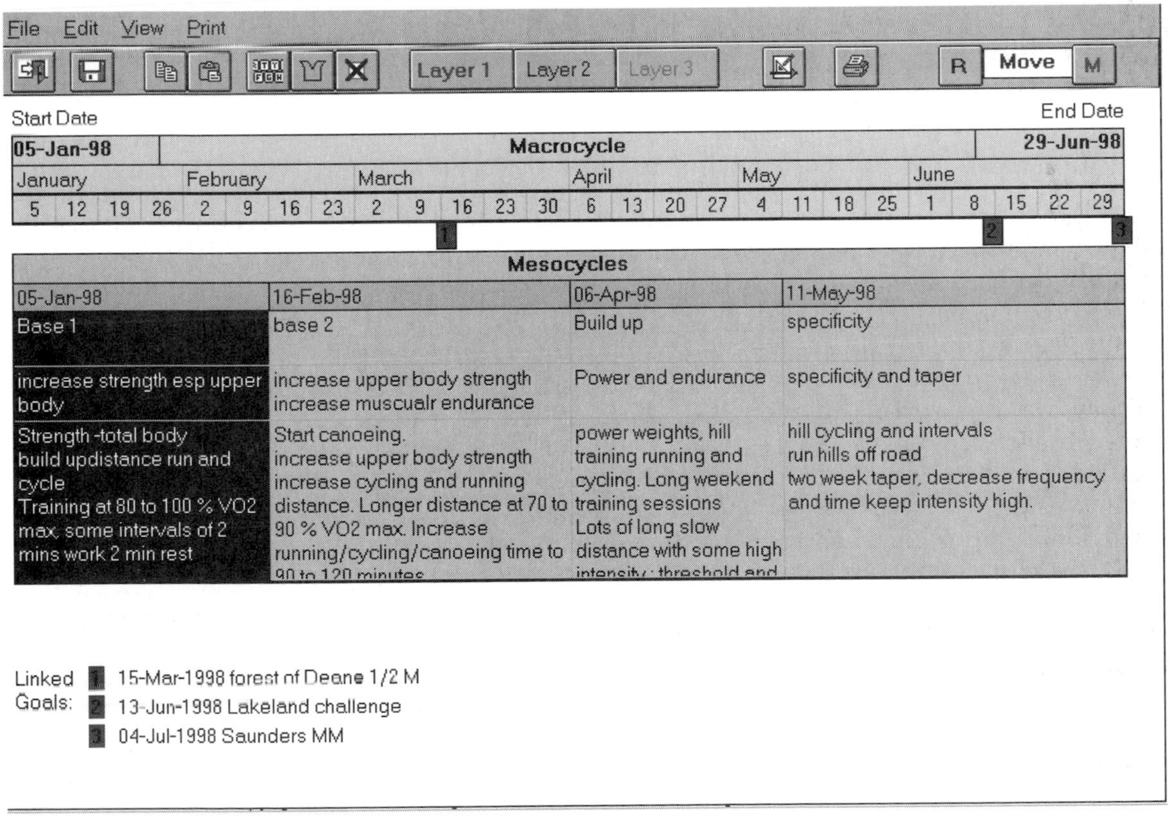

| File | Edit | View | Print | | | | | Layer 1 | Layer 2 | Layer 3 | | | | R | Move | M |

Start Date															End Date	
05-Jan-98					Macrocycle										29-Jun-98	
January			February			March			April		May			June		
5	12	19	26	2	9	16	23	2	9	16	23	30	6	13	20	27	4	11	18	25	1	8	15	22	29

Mesocycles			
05-Jan-98	16-Feb-98	06-Apr-98	11-May-98
Base 1	base 2	Build up	specificity
increase strength esp upper body	increase upper body strength increase muscualr endurance	Power and endurance	specificity and taper
Strength -total body build updistance run and cycle	Start canoeing. increase upper body strength increase cycling and running distance. Longer distance at 70 to 90 % VO2 max. Increase running/cycling/canoeing time to 90 to 120 minutes.	power weights, hill training running and cycling. Long weekend training sessions Lots of long slow distance with some high intensity; threshold and	hill cycling and intervals run hills off road two week taper, decrease frequency and time keep intensity high.
Training at 80 to 100 % VO2 max, some intervals of 2 mins work 2 min rest			

Linked Goals:
1 15-Mar-1998 forest of Deane 1/2 M
2 13-Jun-1998 Lakeland challenge
3 04-Jul-1998 Saunders MM

Figure 18.10 This adventure athlete is competing in a race involving canoeing, cycling, and a fell run race. Her first two mesocycles aim to improve strength and endurance, then she will add power, and finally train specifically for the event

Whatever training is included it has to fit into everyday life. Athletes with the ability to devote their life to training are rare, especially in events which don't attract large sponsorship and prize money, thus lifestyle restraints such as working hours, free time, family responsibilities, etc. may limit the time available to devote to training. This makes it all the more important to ensure that the training programme is designed well.

1   McFarland, E.G. and Wasik, M. (1996) *Injuries in female collegiate swimmers due to swimming and cross training.* Clinical Journal of Sport Medicine (USA) 6/3

2   Ruby, B., Robergs, R., Leadbetter, G., Mermier, C., Chick, T. and Stark, D. (1996) *Cross-training between cycling and running in untrained females.* Journal of Sports Medicine and Physical Fitness (Italy) 36/4

Chapter 19

More is Not Always Better

◆ Progressive overload ◆

OPINION

More training does not always mean better performance.

Rest is an integral part of training. Many athletes forget that the harder you train, the more you must rest to recover, relatively speaking. Exactly how much rest you need will partly depend on your training status and partly on your individual response to training. However, training too much in terms of volume, frequency or intensity leads to poor performance and eventually to overtraining syndrome and illness or injury. To avoid overtraining, the principles of progressive overload should be followed.

OPINION

Don't increase training by more than 10% per week.

Increasing the volume or intensity of training too much will be detrimental to performance and lead eventually to a chronic state of fatigue and to ill health. To ensure that this does not happen many athletes alternate one

Microcycles				
22-Jul-96 (7 weeks)	**skill**			
skill aerobic base/anaerobic recovery strength	skill training x 3 per week aerobic base -run /swim interval/fartlek runs weights			
29-Jul-96	05-Aug-96	12-Aug-96	19-Aug-96	26-Aug-96
7 days	7 days	7 days	7 days	7 days
swim easy x1 run times 1 steady state run times 1 anaerobic intervals weights times 2 skate training x 2	swim easy x1 run times 1 steady state run times 1 anaerobic intervals weights times 2 skate training x 2 swim tri	swim easy x1 run times 1 steady state run times 1 anaerobic intervals weights times 2 skate training x 2	easy week ultra fit rowing competition	swim easy x1 run times 1 steady state run times 1 anaerobic intervals weights times 2 skate training x 2

Figure 19.1 By planning mesocycles and microcycles it is easy to ensure that an easy week is regularly built into a programme

week of hard training and one week of easy training. Others work on two-week cycles. Some progressively overload for four or five weeks and then have an easy week.

Remember overload can occur by increasing volume, or intensity or both. The general stresses of daily life add to the stress of training and may increase the risk of overtraining. An athlete who is working hard at a stressful job, or is suffering from lack of sleep or lack of time to prepare food, runs a higher risk of becoming injured or overtrained. An athlete who is simply tired will, however, recover very quickly with a few days rest, whereas overtraining syndrome is characterised by a sudden decline in performance that takes some time to remedy.

◆ Tapering ◆

Coming up to an event you need to reduce training levels, that is you need to taper. How long the taper is will depend on the scale of the event. A long event will need a long taper, some trainers suggest as much as a four-week taper for a marathon.

When tapering it is best to taper the volume of training rather than the intensity.

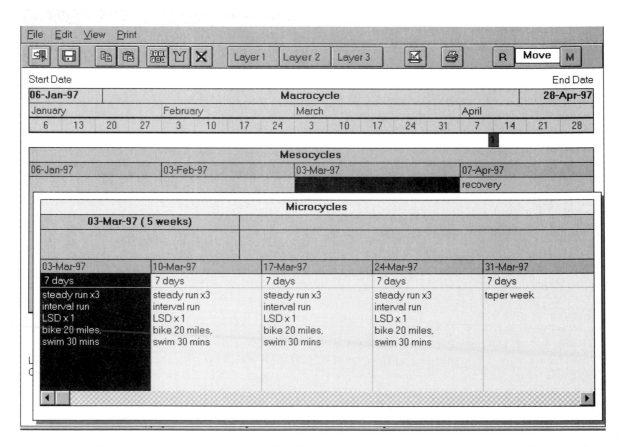

Figure 19.2 Tapering before a race allows for full recovery from training sessions and replenishment of glycogen stores in preparation for the race

♦ Overtraining ♦ syndrome

If overtraining continues it may progress to chronic stage. The signs of overtraining syndrome are as follows:

- decline in performance
- loss of muscle strength
- loss of co-ordination
- decline in maximal work capacity
- decreased appetite
- loss of weight
- occasional nausea
- muscle tenderness
- minor infections
- allergies
- elevated resting heart rate
- elevated blood pressure.

As you will see, many of these signs could occur for other reasons. To complicate matters further, individual athletes will respond differently to overtraining, they will not all exhibit the same combination of symptoms nor in the same order of appearance.

OPINION

The first sign of overtraining is usually decreased performance. Other reliable indicators are heart rate and blood lactate responses to a standard bout of training.

For example, if a particular cycle ride normally takes you 30 minutes to complete with a heart rate of around 170, but starts taking 32 minutes with a heart rate of 175–180 this should alert you to look at your training and see if you are building in enough rest or if you are overloading. You should also examine your training if your rate of perceived exertion goes up for a standard training session.

♦ Injury ♦

Increasing the level of training too much also increases the risk of injury. Injuries may be due to trauma, such as a fall or collision, or may be due to overuse.

Overuse injuries often occur when a sudden change is made to the training, such as a rapid increase in volume or intensity or when the training terrain alters suddenly. Often injuries occur if too much of the training is changed at once, for example adding in hill training, adding in weight training and increasing the volume of training all together.

OPINION

Change only one part of the training at a time.

RICE

Treatment of injury is always RICE.

FACT

Rest the injured area.
Ice or cool the injured area.
Compression using a bandage or tubigrip.
Elevation by raising the injured area up, if possible to heart level.

If this first aid treatment is promptly applied and the help of a medical professional is promptly sought, most soft tissue injuries can be healed relatively quickly. Problems usually occur when the athlete tries to work through the injury or pain.

Cross training and injury

When injury occurs, cross training allows the athlete to continue training by working around the injury. One of my clients, a runner who sustained a stress fracture in the foot, continued training by cycling and swimming and found that he enjoyed it so much that he branched out into triathlon.

By using cross training modes it is possible to maintain fitness while recovering from injury, and also to use cross training itself to aid with strengthening and flexibility work in order to rehabilitate fully. Even when using cross training, however, progression to full training after injury should be gradual if the injury is not to become recurrent.

Chapter 20

Eating Right

Muscles need fuel. To move we must utilise energy, and to replace the energy we use we must eat. Also, training causes damage to our muscles and puts extra strain on the body in general, so that we need to rebuild and repair. If we have broken down the body tissues with training they can become stronger and more able to cope following repair, if we feed them the right ingredients. If we fail to eat well then we are more likely to become ill or injured. Good nutrition is the perfect partner to a good training programme.

♦ What do I need ♦ to eat?

A balance of nutrients is important for both health and fitness training. The body will continue to function reasonably normally for a short while with a dietary imbalance of such nutrients as minerals and vitamins, however eventually the imbalance will make itself known. For nutrients such as carbohydrates and water the effects of deficiency are acute. For the active individual, a basic understanding of good nutritional principles is therefore vital.

A balanced diet

To obtain a healthy balance of carbohydrates, fats and proteins, and to ensure an adequate intake of vitamins, minerals and trace elements, we should attempt to eat more starchy carbohydrate foods such as bread, cereals and rice, more fresh fruit and vegetables, and less fatty foods. The US Department of Health and Human Service published a food pyramid which depicts a base of starchy foods and suggests that oils, fats and sweets should be used sparingly.

However many calories you consume in a day, the balance of foodstuffs within that calorie allowance should remain the same, with most calories coming from complex carbohydrate foods.

For most generally active individuals a well balanced diet following these guidelines will be adequate for whatever activity they do. For those people training more seriously, either for an extreme challenge or for a competitive event, more careful attention to the food they eat is advantageous.

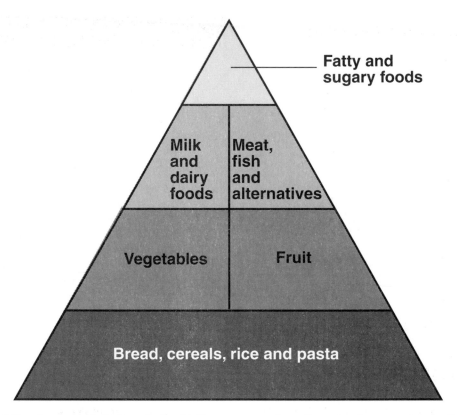

Figure 20.1 Food pyramid: take substantially more servings from food groups towards the bottom of the pyramid

◆ Protein ◆

Protein comes from both animal and vegetable sources and is made up amino acids which are often thought of as the building blocks of the body. Amino acids are rather like the letters of the alphabet, by putting them together in various sequences we can make words, or in the case of amino acids, by putting them together in various sequences we can make different proteins. Protein is found in hormones, enzymes, blood and all body tissues, thus it is very important to us.

In the alphabet there are five vowels. Without these vowels we cannot make words. In the alphabet of amino acids there are eight essential amino acids without which we cannot make proteins. All eight of the essential amino acids are found in animal proteins such as milk, eggs, cheese and meats. However, to achieve a full complement of essential amino acids from vegetable sources we need to combine our protein sources by mixing grains with pulses, or mixing grains with nuts. Therefore grains such as bread, rice and pasta can be mixed with beans and legumes or with nuts and seeds in order to reach a full amino acid complement.

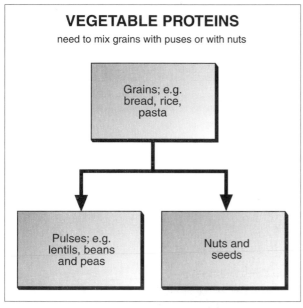

VEGETABLE PROTEINS

need to mix grains with puses or with nuts

Grains; e.g. bread, rice, pasta

Pulses; e.g. lentils, beans and peas

Nuts and seeds

Figure 20.2 Vegetable proteins

♦ Fat ♦

Many people mistakenly think that they should cut out fat from their diet completely, however the body needs fats as a valuable source of energy, to supply and store the fat soluble vitamins, A, D, E and K, and to supply essential fatty acids without which we cannot function healthily.

Because fat makes food palatable and fills us up we add it to all sorts of refined food-stuffs, the result is often a diet too rich in fat. This type of diet has been linked to increased levels of obesity and disease, with the result that we in the western world are encouraged to reduce the amount of fat in our diets.

INTEREST

We still need some fat in our diets, though recommendations are that to remain healthy no more than 33% of calories should come from fat.

♦ Carbohydrate ♦

Carbohydrate foods, often described as the sugary and starchy foods, are the main source of energy for all activities. If carbohydrate intake is low then blood glucose levels drop and muscle glycogen levels become depleted. Carbohydrate is the only energy source for the brain and central nervous system. Low blood glucose levels affect the ability to concentrate and there is evidence that when carbohydrate intake is low, co-ordination is impaired and accidents and injuries occur more frequently.

When blood glucose levels drop we start to feel irritable, weak, shaky and unable to concentrate. Tests also show that reaction time is impaired when carbohydrate levels are low.

How much of each group should I eat?

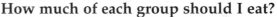
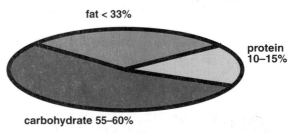

fat < 33%

protein 10–15%

carbohydrate 55–60%

Figure 20.3 Recommended proportion of each food group in the diet

Guidelines vary from country to country and year to year, but generally health guidelines agree that for an active individual the proportions of fat, carbohydrate and protein consumed should be divided by the kcals that they supply. Not more than 33% of kcals should come from fat, 10–15% of kcals should come from protein, and the remaining 55–60% of kcals should come from carbohydrate sources.

How do I know how many kcals I eat from each food group?

Foods supply different amounts of energy per gram depending on the make-up of the food. Fat is very energy-dense and supplies about 9kcals per gram, while protein and carbohydrate each supply around 4kcals per gram. Thus to work out how many kcals of a food come from fat, carbohydrate and protein, simply multiply the total number of grams by the energy from that foodstuff.

For example, if a food is made up of 20g of fat, 60g of carbohydrate and 20g of protein and has 500kcals per 100g then:

20g of fat = 20 x 9kcals = 180 kcals
180/360 x 100 = 36
Thus in this foodstuff 36% of the kcals come from fat.

20g of protein = 20 x 4kcals = 80kcals
80/360 x 100 = 16
Thus in this foodstuff 16% of the kcals come from protein.

60g of carbohydrate = 60 x 4kcals = 240kcals
240/360 x 100 = 48
Thus in this foodstuff 48% of the kcals come from carbohydrate.

Overall, you should eat foods that are less than 33% fat and have a high carbohydrate content.

Of course if you work all of this out for everything you eat you have no time left for training. Simply following the food pyramid and being a little stricter on your fat consumption while enjoying complex carbohydrates and vegetables should be sufficient to balance your diet and still leave you with plenty of time to train.

♦ Weight loss ♦

A very simple formula should help us with this apparently complex area.

FACT

- Calories in > calories out = weight gain
- Calories out > calories in = weight loss

Calorie requirements are different for everyone depending on genetics, age, gender, lean body mass, and current activity level. To lose weight we must expend more calories in daily living and activity than we take in as food. Put simply, to lose weight we must eat less, exercise more, or better still combine both.

To lose one pound of fat, we need to create an energy deficit of 3,500 calories.

Over a week this amounts to creating an energy deficit of 500 calories per day.

FACT

3,500 calories/7 days per week = 500 calories per day

This means we need to eat 500 calories less per day in order to lose one pound of fat per week, however by combining diet and exercise we could lose the same amount of weight by eating just 250 calories less and expending 250 calories in exercise per day. Attempting to lose more weight than one to two pounds a week is not advised. Where more weight loss than this occurs it is often due to a loss of muscle mass as well as fat mass.

When calorie restriction is severe the resultant deficit in carbohydrate intake causes low muscle glycogen levels and low blood glucose levels, predisposing the athlete to fatigue and injury. Also, carbohydrate is always stored alongside water – one molecule of carbohydrate with three molecules of water – thus some of the apparent weight loss that occurs with severe calorie restriction is due to glycogen and associated water loss, rather than fat loss. In addition, the fatigue caused by low glycogen levels mean that it is difficult to increase energy expenditure through training. Finally, during severe calorie restriction exercise is partially fuelled by protein taken from broken down muscle, thus some of the weight loss is muscle rather than fat.

Weight loss and cross training

When we train for single sport events we are limited to how much repetition the body can take before overuse injuries start to occur. By cross training we can increase energy expenditure by training for longer duration or more often, without subjecting the body to the same risk of overuse injuries.

♦ More about ♦ carbohydrate

OPINION

Base your meals around carbohydrates rather than proteins. Think: what carbohydrate am I going to eat, will it be bread, rice or pasta? Now what vegetables shall I put with it? Finally, what protein shall I add?

Carbohydrate is necessary in order to utilise fat as fuel. In prolonged endurance activity, when carbohydrate levels are depleted we do not immediately utilise fat as fuel but start to fuel the exercise by breaking down our body proteins. We use our own muscle to fuel the exercise. Thus carbohydrate is protein-sparing. The greater the carbohydrate stores the less likely we are to use muscle protein to fuel long duration exercise.

The amount of glycogen stored in the muscles is directly related to dietary carbohydrate intake, however even a well nourished human being can only store about 1,500–2,000kcals of carbohydrate. We therefore need to regularly replace our carbohydrate stores by ensuring that a large percentage of the calories we eat come from carbohydrate foods. In most western diets only about 40% of the total kcals are obtained from such sources, yet recommendations for athletes are that up to 70% of the calories should be obtained from carbohydrate.

Studies also show that for athletes training one to two hours a day, muscle glycogen levels drop dramatically over a week if carbohydrate intake is normal, that is around 40%, but drop much less on a high carbohydrate diet.

Added to this it is advantageous to refuel with carbohydrate immediately after exercise, as at this time the muscle is particularly receptive to taking on glycogen and supercompensates, increasing the amount of glycogen stored. It is recommended that you should eat at least one-and-a-half grams of carbohydrate per kilogram of body weight within 30 minutes of completing exercise, thus a 70kg person should eat at least 105g of carbohydrate within 30 minutes of stopping exercise. This could be two bananas and three sweet biscuits, or a potato and baked beans. As water is taken into the muscle along with carbohydrate the athlete should also remain fully hydrated.

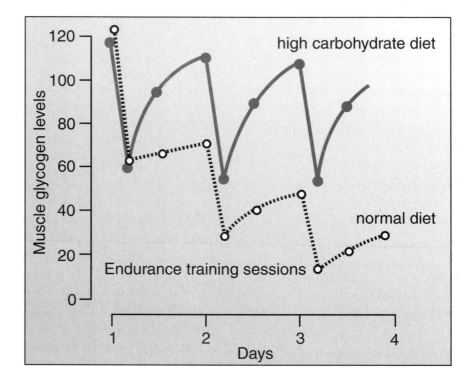

Figure 20.4 This graph shows the reduction in muscle glycogen levels when endurance training every day on a high carbohydrate diet (70%) and on a normal diet (40%)

Glycaemic index

The form in which you ingest carbohydrate makes a difference to how quickly it is synthesised in the body. Carbohydrates can be classed by glycaemic index (GI), those with a high glycaemic index being absorbed quickly and those with a low glycaemic index more slowly. It is thought that eating foods with a low glycaemic index 30–60 minutes before exercise may maintain a higher blood sugar level during exercise and increase the concentration of fatty acids in the blood, thus improving fat oxidation and reducing reliance on carbohydrate to fuel the exercise. After exercise, high glycaemic index foods may restore muscle glycogen more efficiently.

Foods with a high glycaemic index

	amount for 50g of carbohydrate
sucrose	50g
honey	67g
maple syrup	80g
bread	4 slices (28g each)
bread sticks	7 sticks
wholewheat sweet biscuits	3 biscuits
cornflakes	59g
muesli	6 tbsps (70g)
shredded wheat	3 pieces
weetabix	4 pieces
raisins	78g
banana	2 (120g each)
potato baked	1 potato (200g)
potato boiled	254g
sweetcorn	219g

Foods with a low glycaemic index

	amount for 50g of carbohydrate
apple	2.5 (138g each)
cherries	44 cherries
dates	8 dates
figs	5 figs (fresh, 50g each)
grapefruit	2.5 grapefruits (118g each)
peach	5 peaches (90g each)
pear	2 pears (166g each)
plum	5.5 plums (66g each)
butter beans	292g
kidney beans	220g
chickpeas	305g
green beans	630g
green peas	345g
red lentils	294g
skimmed milk	995ml
yoghurt	658ml

Table adapted from *The Complete Book of Sports Nutrition* by Anita Bean (A & C Black)

Foods with a moderate glycaemic index

	amount for 50g of carbohydrate
spaghetti/macaroni	198g (cooked)
noodles	370g (cooked)
whole grain rye bread	4 slices (28g each)
rice (white)	169g (cooked)
grapes	323g
orange (navel)	3 oranges (140g each)
yams (boiled or baked)	168g
baked beans	485g

For endurance events lasting several hours, such as ironman triathlon, mountain marathon or challenge events, and for stop-and-go sports run as all day or multi-day tournaments, the athlete should refuel with carbohydrates during the event or between games in the tournament. Again, carbohydrates with a high to moderate glycaemic index are useful.

◆ More about fat ◆

Fat is a vital part of hormones and of the insulation around nerve fibres, vital organs and cell membranes. Deficiency in certain fatty acids causes ill health. Fats are made up of high-density lipoproteins (HDL), low-density lipoproteins (LDL), and very low-density lipoproteins (VLDL). Low-density lipoproteins and very low-density lipoproteins are largely found in animal fats and are solid at room temperature, while high-density lipoproteins are largely found in vegetable fats and are liquid at room temperature. High total dietary fat intake is a risk factor in coronary heart disease, and a high dietary intake of low density lipoproteins within a moderate total fat intake is also detrimental to health, thus, wherever possible, fat from vegetable sources should be utilised in preference to animal fats.

Fat as fuel

Fat is very energy-dense and as such is a useful fuel. About 50,000–60,000kcal of energy are stored as fat in the adipose tissue of the body.

Fat is made up of fatty acids and glycerol stored as triglyceride. As well as being stored in the adipose tissue, triglyceride is stored as tiny droplets in the muscle fibres, and is known as intramuscular triglyceride. Intramuscular triglyceride provides 2,000–3,000kcal of stored energy, far more energy than is stored as muscle glycogen.

Both triglyceride from adipose tissue and intramuscular triglyceride is oxidised to provide energy. As exercise intensity increases from low to moderate intensity, the rate of fat oxidation from adipose tissue declines, but due to a relatively large use of intramuscular triglyceride the rate of total fat oxidation increases. Endurance training increases the body's ability to utilise intramuscular triglyceride as fuel. However, in comparison to carbohydrate stored as muscle glycogen, fat stores are mobilised and oxidised at relatively slow rates during exercise.

The fat burning myth

At 25% VO$_2$max, almost all of the energy expenditure during exercise is fuelled by fat, whereas at 65% VO$_2$max only 50% of energy expenditure is fuelled by fat. It is therefore often assumed that the intensity of exercise must be kept low in order to burn fat. However, expressing energy derived from fat as a percentage of energy expenditure without considering total energy expenditure is misleading. Because the total rate of energy expenditure is greater at 65% VO$_2$max, the absolute rate of fat oxidation is greater than at 25% VO$_2$max.

Ultimately, reductions in body fat as a result of long term exercise depend on the total daily energy expenditure and the total daily energy input, rather than on the actual fuel oxidised during exercise

◆ Calcium and iron and ◆ the female athlete

In an attempt to keep their body weight down many female endurance athletes reduce their calorie intake. Some do not eat enough to meet the recommended dietary allowance (RDA) of calories for inactive women of the same age. Low calorie intake is often associated with reduced levels of vitamins and minerals in the diet, thus female athletes who compromise their nutritional status in this way may be deficient in vital nutrients.

One such nutrient is calcium. As ready sources of calcium such as milk and cheese also have a high fat content, athletes concerned about their weight may cut out these foods. Low calcium levels are associated with stress fractures and with osteoporosis or brittle bone disease, therefore calcium levels should be maintained by eating calcium-rich foods; where a reduction in fat intake is desirable low fat dairy products should be added to the diet.

Because of menstrual blood loss, an inadequate diet may also lead to poor iron levels, iron-deficient anaemia, and consequently poor performance in endurance sports where the oxygen-carrying capacity of the blood is compromised.

---

1 Maughan, R. (1993) *Nutrition*. Gatorade Sports Science Exchange, vol. 4, no. 4

Chapter 21

Drinking Right

◆ Water ◆

About 60% of our body weight is made up of water, yet even at rest we lose about 2.3 litres of fluid per day through evaporation from the skin and respiratory tract and through excretion. During heavy exercise in heat that fluid loss may reach two to three litres per hour.[1]

Unless we make concerted efforts to replace fluid loss while exercising we will become dehydrated. Even slight dehydration is detrimental to performance. For each litre of water lost, heart rate increases by about eight beats per minute, cardiac output declines by 1l/min, and core body temperature rises by 0.3°C. Studies have shown that even a 2% dehydration, when measured by body weight, decreases performance by 6–7%[2]; dehydration of about 4% will produce a decline in performance of 20–30%.

◆ Drinking before ◆ exercise

Despite evidence supporting the need to be well hydrated prior to exercise, many people start training in a dehydrated state.

> ### QUOTE
> The American College of Sports Medicine recommend that 'individuals drink about 500ml (about 17oz) of fluid about two hours before exercising to promote adequate hydration.'[3]

However, it takes a concerted effort and is not generally habitual to drink this much fluid even prior to exercise. In addition, many people only think about taking on fluid if they are going to exercise in the heat or if the exercise is going to be intense. Yet fluid loss enough to affect performance occurs even in a cold environment, and many studies show that during long duration, low- to moderate-intensity exercise such as walking, dehydration is a limiting factor and affects both performance and rate of perceived exertion.

◆ Drinking during ◆ exercise

Having made the effort to be well hydrated prior to exercise it is important that during exercise we consciously take on fluid to ensure that we remain so, especially for sessions lasting over an hour or if exercising in the heat.

Start drinking before you feel thirsty and if possible take small amounts of fluid every few minutes. Many studies show that we have to re-educate ourselves to stay adequately hydrated during exercise; if we drink only when we feel thirsty it is unlikely that we will remain hydrated. Sometimes people say that drinking during exercise makes them feel sick. It is likely that this is because even a small degree of dehydration upsets the gastric tract causing feelings of nausea and bloatedness. To overcome this it is important to start exercising well hydrated and to continue taking on fluids during the early stages of exercise. To remember to do this may take practice.

♦ Drinking after ♦ exercise

It is unlikely that we will remain fully hydrated during long duration exercise or exercise in the heat, so we need to rehydrate after we finish exercising. For multi-sport athletes who are completing more than one training session per day, or for tournaments where more than one game is played per day, it is vital that the athlete should rehydrate between sessions or between games.

♦ What should I ♦ drink

It is often supposed that drinking plain water is best. Plain water is indeed good, however because it removes the osmotic drive to drink it may result in thirst being satisfied before adequate fluid has been ingested.[4] The presence of low levels of sodium chloride and of other electrolytes have been shown to promote greater fluid intake. For this reason a range of isotonic electrolyte replacement drinks have become available, some ready-mixed and some in powder form that need

preparing. When using electrolyte replacement drinks it is important that they are prepared according to the directions or they may reduce fluid absorption.

Carbohydrate drinks

For long duration exercise which drains the carbohydrate reserves, replacing some of the carbohydrate along with fluid replacement can significantly enhance performance. Most research into carbohydrate replacement drinks has focused on long duration endurance exercise, however more recent studies have provided evidence that shorter duration and high-intensity, intermittent exercise also benefits from carbohydrate replacement.[5]

As with electrolyte drinks, carbohydrate drinks should be prepared following the instructions. Too strong a solution will impair fluid absorption and promote dehydration.

---

1 Wilmore, J. and Costill, D. *Physiology of Sport and Exercise*. Human Kinetics. pp 363–5

2 Armstrong, L.E., Costill, D.L. and Fink, W.J. (1985) *Influence of diuretic-induced dehydration on competitive running performance*. Med. Sci. Sport and Exerc. 17: 456–61

3 American College of Sports Medicine (1996). *Position stand on exercise and fluid replacement*. Med. Sci. Sport and Exerc. 28: i–vii.

4 Costill, D.L., and Sparks, K.E. (1973) *Rapid fluid replacement following thermal dehydration*. J. Appl. Physiol. 34: 299–303.

5 Murray, B. (1996) *Fluid Replacement: The American College of Sports Medicine Position Stand*. GSSE#63-vol. 9, no 4 (supplement)

Appendix

♦ Exercise test I ♦

The usefulness of exercise tests is dependent on the person being tested and the ability of the tester. The major reason for carrying out an exercise test is to find useful information about your state of fitness. One test that is useful to many endurance athletes measures anaerobic threshold.

Pre-test conditions

For all tests:

- ensure you have not eaten, smoked, or drunk tea or coffee for at least two hours before the test
- do not take part if you are recovering from illness or have a cold, or if you are taking beta blocker drugs which will depress heart rate scores
- wear loose-fitting, comfortable clothing.

Pulse rate deflection point – for anaerobic threshold

Training at or just below anaerobic threshold (threshold training) can be achieved by using a heart rate monitor if the athlete knows what their heart rate is at threshold level.

This can be tested for in a laboratory and many sports science laboratories allied to universities will, for a fee, test an athlete. Alternatively, a field test can be used.

It has been observed that when work rate, as measured by power output, is increased in regular increments the heart rate increases linearly, up to a point at which power output continues to increase but heart rate plateaus or even drops off. This point is known as the pulse rate deflection point or heart rate deflection point, and corresponds to anaerobic threshold or OBLA. This heart rate can then be used as a reference point for threshold training.

Retesting will give an indication of whether training is achieving a higher threshold. If on retest a higher pulse rate deflection point is reached, this indicates that the athlete is capable of supplying energy aerobically at a higher intensity of exercise.

Please note, this is a maximum test and as such carries high risk. It should only be done under medical supervision and should not be done with individuals who are new to exercise or have any contra-indications.

Cyclists – bike ergometer

1 Warm up thoroughly for 15–30 minutes.
2 Use a moderately large gear.
3 Ride as close to racing position as possible.
4 Once warmed up, reach a comfortable pedal cadence (70–80rpm).
5 Maintain this cadence throughout the test.
6 For less well trained cyclists, start at 150 watts.
7 For well trained cyclists, start at 200 watts.
8 Every minute, increase the watts by 10–15 watts.
9 Keep pedal cadence constant.
10 At the end of each minute record the heart rate.
11 The test is ended when the person cannot do the task any longer.

Following the exercise:

- plot a graph of workload in watts (x axis) against heart rate (y axis)
- record the pedal frequency
- record the duration of the warm-up
- record the duration of the test
- record the gear used
- record maximum pulse rate reached
- record maximum wattage reached
- record pulse rate deflection point. This is the point at which the linear correlation between pulse rate and wattage is lost.

Ensure when retesting that the same conditions are used, e.g. pedal cadence, warm-up period etc.

Runners – treadmill

A similar method may be used for runners using a treadmill, increasing the workload by increasing the incline in regular increments.

1 Warm up thoroughly for 15–30 minutes.

2 Once warmed up, run at comfortably fast pace.
3 Maintain this pace throughout the test.
4 Every two minutes, or when heart rate reaches steady state increase the incline by 1%.
5 Keep the pace constant.
6 At the end of each minute record the heart rate.
7 The test is ended when the person cannot do the task any longer.

Following the exercise:

- plot a graph of workload in incline (x axis) against heart rate (y axis)
- record the pace
- record the duration of the warm-up
- record the duration of the test
- record maximum pulse rate reached
- record maximum incline reached
- record pulse rate deflection point. This is the point at which the linear correlation between pulse rate and incline is lost.

Ensure when retesting that the same conditions are used, e.g. pace, warm-up period etc.

♦ Exercise test II ♦

Measurement of body fat

Many athletes wish to reduce body fat levels to aid performance, so they look for a club or laboratory that will measure body fat and compare this to the body fat typical of top level athletes.

Skin fold measurements

One of the most common methods of estimating body fat is by using skin fold measurements. This method measures folds of skin along with the underlying subcutaneous fat at various sites on the body, and then uses regression equations to estimate total fat from these measurements.

To be accurate:

- the skin fold calliper pressure should not vary by more than 2 g•mm^{-2} over a range of 2–40mm and should be 9–20 g•mm^{-2}.[1]
- the skin fold sites must be determined using anatomic reference points
- the measurement should be read no more than two seconds after applying the full force of the calliper.

Problems occur because of:

- an error on behalf of the person measuring
- difficulty in measuring obese individuals
- poor quality or badly maintained callipers
- assumptions made when preparing the equations used to determine percentage body fat from the sum of the skin fold sites.

For example, the assumption is made that in young adult individuals subcutaneous fat amounts to 50% of total body fat and that distribution is consistent between people. As ageing occurs less fat is deposited subcutaneously and more intra-abdominal fat is present, thus a scale which takes into account the ageing process is used. How much of body composition changes are due to ageing and how much are due to lack of activity is at present undetermined, therefore whether this scale is accurate for very active or highly fit older individuals is questionable.

Bio electrical impedence

A relatively economical and increasingly popular method of estimating body fat is by the use of bio electrical impedence. This is based on the concept that electric flow through hydrated fat free tissue and extra cellular water meets less resistance than through fat tissue. Thus impedence to the flow of electricity will be directly related to the amount of fatty tissue.

Because hydration affects the normal concentrations of electrolytes in the body the accuracy of this method will be affected by either overhydration or dehydration. Dehydration will decrease the impedence measure to yield a lower percentage of fat, while overhydration will have the opposite effect.[2] This has implications when measuring female subjects who may retain large amounts of fluid during the luteal phase of the menstrual cycle. Skin temperature may also affect readings.

◆ Exercise test III ◆

Height and weight

Body stature and girth measurements, although often used in isolation, may be especially useful when used in conjunction with the sum of skin fold sites as in the Canadian Standardised Fitness Test, in which body mass index (BMI) is calculated by dividing body weight in kilograms by height in metres squared, and is reviewed alongside the sum of five skin fold measurements to determine whether a high BMI is due to excess adiposity or to muscularity. The body fat distribution is then also determined using waist to hip ratio and the sum of two skin folds taken at the sites of the iliac crest and sub-scapular.[3]

1 Skinner, J.S., Baldini, F.D. and Gardener, A.W. (1990) *Assessment of Fitness in Exercise*.

2 McArdle, Katch and Katch. *Exercise and Work Physiology*. Lea and Febiger. p. 623

3 Gledhill, N. (1990) Discussion: Assessment of Fitness. In *Exercise, Fitness and Health*. Ed. by Bouchard, C., Shepherd, R., Stephens, T., Sutton, J.R. and McPherson, B.D. Human Kinetics. p. 122

Glossary

1RM – one repetition maximum. The resistance needed to limit the lifter to one repetition only. A second repetition of the exercise cannot be achieved.

Actin filaments – *see* myofilaments.

Active lifestyle – a lifestyle incorporating physical activity. Physical activities include walking or cycling to the shops instead of using the car, walking upstairs instead of taking the elevator, climbing on to chairs or steps to reach things in high cupboards or reaching down for things in low cupboards instead of storing things within easy reach, etc.

Active living – as defined by Fitness Canada 1991: 'A way of life in which physical activity is valued and integrated into daily life.'

Active range of movement – the range of movement when only the muscles effecting that movement are used.

Acute – of a rapid onset and short duration.

Adenosine di-phosphate (ADP) – when the high energy bond in adenosine tri-phosphate (ATP) is broken, adenosine di-phosphate (ADP) and one free phosphate molecule is formed.

Adenosine tri-phosphate (ATP) – made up of one molecule of adenosine and three phosphate molecules attached by high energy bonds. Energy is trapped inside these bonds.

Aerobic power (VO_2max) – the maximum amount of oxygen that you can extract from the air and utilise in the working muscles for the aerobic production of energy.

Alveolar – small airsacs in the lungs, the site of pulmonary gaseous exchange.

Anabolism – the building up of muscle tissue. The constructive phase of metabolism.

Anaerobic glycolysis – utilises carbohydrate stored in the body as glycogen, converting it into glucose and then into a substance called pyruvate.

Anaerobic threshold – also called onset of blood lactate accumulation (OBLA) or lactate threshold. The workload at which lactate production is greater than lactate removal and so lactate builds up to a level such that muscular contraction is interfered with.

Arteries – carry blood away from the heart

Biomechanics – an application of the principles of mechanics to human or animal movement.

Biopsies – a needle with a canula is inserted into the muscle tissue and a small piece of muscle tissue is withdrawn.

Blood lipids – fats such as triglycerides, high-density lipoproteins (HDL), low-density lipoproteins (LDL) and very low-density lipoproteins (VLDL) circulating in the blood plasma.

Blood plasma – fluid portion of the blood.

Bronchial tubes – portion of the tubular airways leading into the alveolar of the lungs.

Capillaries – small blood vessels forming a network throughout the body.

Cardiac drift or **heart rate drift** – with the onset of exercise the heart rate increases from resting level and stabilises, usually changing very little after five to 10 minutes of steady state exercise. However, if exercise continues for a longer period of time, the heart rate continues to rise and is accompanied by a decrease in stroke volume.

Cardiac muscle – the muscle found in the heart.

Cardiac output – the volume of blood pumped out by the heart per minute and is the stroke volume x the heart rate.

Cardio-vascular fitness – a level of aerobic exercise that taxes the cardio-vascular system enough to stimulate physiological adaptation such that it is able to deliver and utilise oxygen sufficiently to fuel prolonged intensive exercise.

Cardio-vascular training (CV) – improves the efficiency of the heart.

Catabolism – the breaking down of muscle tissue. The destructive phase of metabolism.

Cholesterol – a fat that is ingested in the diet and is also produced in the liver. Foods high in cholesterol are derived from animal sources. A high level of cholesterol and especially a high ratio of total cholesterol to high-density lipoproteins is associated with increased risk of atherosclerosis and coronary heart disease.

Chronic – of gradual onset and long duration.

Circuit training – a series of exercises arranged in such a manner that they are each performed for a period of time or a number of repetitions in sequence in order to create a complete workout.

COH – chemical symbol for carbohydrate.

Competition – competition phase, within which the competition or series of competitions take place. The athlete must peak and retain form.

Concentration gradient – gases diffuse from high concentration to low concentration along a concentration gradient.

Concentric – during a concentric contraction the two ends of the muscle move closer together and the muscle length shortens.

Conditioning – when elements of fitness such as strength and endurance are trained.

Contra-indicated exercise – exercises that are not recommended for a particular client because of previous injury, present medical condition or his/her particular biomechanics.

Coronary heart disease (CHD) – a disease of the coronary arteries, i.e. those supplying the heart, in which they become narrowed and in the worst cases completely occluded. If a primary artery is occluded and no alternative route is available, that part of the myocardium normally supplied by that artery cannot function and a myocardial infarction or heart attack occurs. Characteristics known to increase the probability of developing coronary heart disease include cigarette smoking, elevated blood lipids (LDL to HDL ratio), inactivity, hypertension, family history of heart disease, psychological stress and obesity.

Creatine-phosphate – stored in the muscles and broken down to release energy. It is very responsive to the needs of the muscles and is capable of supplying energy very quickly but only for an extremely short period of time.

Diastole – resting phase or relaxation of cardiac muscle that allows the heart to refill with blood, and allows coronary circulation to occur.

Diastolic – the blood pressure measurement during the phase of diastole.

Eccentric – when a muscle is generating force in an attempt to overcome a resistance but is in fact lengthening (giving in to the resistance) it is working in the eccentric phase of the contraction.

Efferent nerves – motor nerves. They transmit messages from the central nervous system out to the body.

Endurance – the ability of a muscle or group of muscles to overcome a resistance for an extended period of time, that is more than once. The ability to perform a physical workload for extended periods of time.

Enzymes – complex proteins formed in living cells which assist chemical processes without being changed themselves, i.e. organic catalysts.

Ergometer – a piece of equipment which is calibrated and produces measurable units of work such that a person's work output can be measured.

Estimated maximum heart rate – maximum heart rate is most often estimated as 220 minus your age. Thus for a person who is 35 their maximum heart rate would be estimated as 185 beats per minute ($220 - 35 = 185$). As this is an estimation it is not accurate, but is used as a safe way of estimating workload.

Fast glycolytic fibres (FG) – may be termed type II fibres. They are well adapted for anaerobic respiration and they reach peak tension very quickly.

Fast oxidative glycolytic (FOG) – may be termed type IIA fibres. Similar to fast glycolytic fibres, but with training they are capable of adapting to aerobic respiration.

FITTA – Frequency, Intensity, Time (volume), Type of exercise, and Adherence can be manipulated to form a training programme specific to an athlete's needs.

Fixator muscles – check unwanted movement in a joint or joint complex.

Force – something that causes an object to be formed or moved.

Forced vital capacity – the amount of air that can be forced out of the lungs in one breath.

Glycogen – the body's store of carbohydrate.

Golgi tendon organs (GTOs) – nerve receptors located within the tendons. Putting tension on a tendon, as may occur during stretch but more often during a muscle contraction, may fire the golgi tendon organ reflex causing the muscle to relax.

H_2O – chemical symbol for water.

Haemoglobin – the iron-containing pigment of red blood cells that carries oxygen in the blood.

HDL to LDL ratio – the ratio of high-density lipoproteins to low-density lipoproteins found circulating in the blood. A high proportion of high-density lipoproteins is associated with a reduced risk of developing atheroma.

High-density lipoprotein (HDL) – lipoprotein contained in blood plasma and composed of a high proportion of protein and a low proportion of triglyceride and cholesterol. A high concentration of HDL is associated with lowered risk of coronary heart disease.

Hormones – chemical messengers produced by the body and transported in the blood to its target tissue.

Hyperextension – overextension of a joint.

Hyperplasia – the theory of hyperplasia states that the muscle fibres themselves split and so extra muscle fibres are created within a single muscle.

Hypertension – raised blood pressure. If resting values are greater than 140mm/90mmHg chronic hypertension exists.

Hypertrophy – the theory of hypertrophy is that the muscle filaments increase in number within each single muscle fibre, thus increasing the cross sectional area of each muscle fibre.

Insulin response – the production of insulin in response to ingestion of carbohydrate. As the body becomes more sensitive to insulin, less insulin is produced by the pancreas.

Insulin sensitivity – the taking up of glucose from the blood by the working muscles and the fat cells in response to output of insulin by the pancreas. As the body becomes fitter the response to insulin becomes more sensitive.

Insulin – hormone produced by the pancreas, used in carbohydrate metabolism and transportation of glucose to the working muscles.

Interval training – consists of intermittent exercise with regular rest periods. The ratio of work to rest is manipulated according to the desired training effect.

Isokinetic contraction – one in which the speed of movement around a joint is controlled by an external force.

Isometric contraction – force is created but no movement across the joint occurs.

Isotonic contraction – one in which there is movement around a joint.

Karvonen formula – MHR – RHR x ?% + RHR = ?% of VO$_2$max.
The following example uses this formula for prescribed exercise intensity for a 35 year old with a resting heart rate of 54 beats per minute, where MHR = maximum heart rate and RHR = resting heart rate:
185 – 54 x 75% + 54 = 152 (heart rate at 75% MHRR).

Lactate – a product of anaerobic metabolism which builds up in the form of lactic acid. **Lactic acid** build-up in the muscle blocks muscle contraction causing a burning sensation and forcing the body to slow down or stop when the intensity of exercise is too high for too long a period of time.

Lactate threshold – also called anaerobic threshold or onset of blood lactate accumulation (OBLA). The workload at which lactate production is greater than lactate removal and so lactate builds up to a level such that muscular contraction is interfered with.

Lactate tolerance – the body's ability to tolerate lactate build-up.

Low-density lipoprotein (LDL) – Lipoprotein contained in blood plasma and composed of a moderate proportion of protein with a high proportion of cholesterol. A high concentration of LDL is associated with an increased risk of coronary heart disease.

Macrocycle – the period of time from now until you reach your main goal.

Maximum heart rate or **peak heart rate** – the maximum heart rate possible for an individual during any given exercise modality.

Maximum heart rate reserve (MHRR) – true maximum heart rate minus true resting heart rate.

Maximum oxygen uptake (VO$_2$max) – is the highest amount of oxygen that the body can consume for the aerobic production of ATP; that is, the amount of oxygen that the body can take in and utilise in the working muscles for the production of energy.

Mesocycles – macrocycles can be split into shorter sections during which you focus on particular elements of training. These shorter sections or phases are called mesocycles.

Metabolic enzyme profile – muscle fibres can be characterised by distinguishing the enzymes characteristic of the different energy systems that they use.

Mitochondria – the sites within the muscle cell where aerobic metabolism, the oxidation of fats and carbohydrate, takes place.

mM = mMols – a measure of blood lactate measured in mMol's per litre. Anaerobic threshold is normally said to be at 4.0 mM/l.

Motor end plate – the interface between the nerve ending and the muscle cell.

Motor unit – each nerve ending serves a number of muscle fibres. The nerve ending and its associated muscle fibres are known collectively as a single motor unit.

Multi-gym – resistance equipment using systems of levers, pulleys and weight stacks.

Muscular endurance – the ability of a muscle or group of muscles to exert force to overcome a resistance for an extended period of time. It is an expression of the ability to repeatedly generate muscular force.

Muscular strength – an expression of the amount of force generated by one single maximum contraction. It refers to the ability of a muscle or group of muscles to exert maximum force to overcome a resistance.

Myocardium – the muscular wall of the heart.

Myofilaments – tiny filaments of proteins called actin and myosin. When a muscle fibre is innervated to contract, these actin and myosin filaments slide across each other causing the muscle to contract. This is known as the sliding filament theory.

Myogenic changes – changes involving an increase in the density or the size of the muscle.

Myoglobin – a pigment found in muscle that transports oxygen from the cell membrane to the mitochondria.

Myosin filaments – *see* myofilaments.

Neurogenic changes – changes happening at a neurogenic level, i.e. within the nerve pathways.

Norm – the average or mean measurement taken from a population.

Obesity – a condition in which a person's body fat percentage is above that which increases risk of disease. Medical opinion is divided over the actual body fat percentages classified as constituting a condition of obesity.

OBLA (onset of blood lactate accumulation) – also known as anaerobic threshold or lactate threshold. The workload at which lactate production is greater than lactate removal and so lactate builds up to a level such that muscular contraction is interfered with.

Occluded – completely blocked.

Olympic weight lifting – strength sport consisting of the combined score from two free weight lifts, the clean and jerk and the snatch.

Osteoporosis – a disease affecting bone density and strength which is reduced such that fractures occur spontaneously or with minor falls and bumps. Sometimes known as brittle bone disease, osteoporosis affects one in four women in Britain by the age of 60 and this becomes one in two by the age of 70. Women are affected more than men due to the loss of the hormone oestrogen after the menopause.

Overload – the body only adapts to unaccustomed demand. To improve fitness you must ask it to do more than it is used to doing.

Oxidative enzymes – the enzymes involved in aerobic metabolism.

Partial pressure – the pressure exerted by individual gases in a mixture of gases.

Passive range of movement – demonstrated when joint movement is assisted by an outside force.

Peak heart rate – maximum heart rate possible for an individual during any given exercise modality.

Periodisation – a method of structuring training in order to prevent overtraining and to optimise peak performance.

Periosteum – the connective tissue sheath wrapped around bone.

Peripheral neuromuscular facilitation (PNF) – stretching utilising the golgi tendon organ (GTO) reflex by purposely putting the tendon under tension thus causing the reflex action of muscle relaxation.

Power – the product of force and velocity, or strength x speed. Power is a product of the speed of contraction and force of contraction, with peak power output generally occurring at around 30% of maximum velocity.

Pyruvate – carbohydrate is broken down into pyruvate which is further broken down to release energy.

RICE – Rest, Ice, Compression, Elevation. A formula for effective first aid in the case of closed soft tissue injuries. In order to reduce swelling, the limb should be rested, ice should be applied, some form of compression should be applied and the limb should be elevated.

Rate of perceived exertion (RPE) – rates the intensity of exercise by how the exercise feels, e.g. 'somewhat hard' , 'easy', 'very hard'.

Reciprocal innervation – any movement involving contracting individual muscle fibres or groups of muscle fibres in the right sequence to cause that movement to happen. Simultaneously opposing muscle fibres must be allowed to relax in order that they do not block that movement from happening.

Repetition maximum (RM) – the greatest resistance that you can overcome for a particular lift. Thus the heaviest weight that can be lifted for 10 repetitions (i.e. an eleventh is not possible) is known as 10 repetitions maximum (10 reps max or 10RM). The heaviest weight that can be lifted for six repetitions is known as 6RM. The maximum for one repetition would be 1RM.

Repetitions – numbers of times of repeating an exercise.

Resting heart rate (RHR) – heart rate taken in the morning after waking up (gently), emptying the bladder and then resting again for a few minutes to allow the heart rate to settle.

SAID principle – Specific Adaptation to Imposed Demand.

Slow oxidative fibres (SO) – may be termed type I fibres. They have a lot of mitochondria and oxidative enzymes and a plentiful supply of capillaries. They are well adapted for aerobic respiration.

Smooth muscle – found in the gastrointestinal tract.

Steady state – occurs when nearly all the cost of the exercise is met by aerobic metabolism.

Strength – the ability of a muscle or group of muscles to overcome a resistance once.

Striated or skeletal muscle – the muscle which is attached to the skeletal system and which is under voluntary control. This is the muscle that we use to maintain posture and effect movement. This is also the muscle that is of importance in relation to fitness, specifically in relation to muscular strength, muscular endurance and power.

Stroke volume – the amount of blood ejected from the left ventricle of the heart during contraction.

Systole – the active phase or contraction of cardiac muscle to expel blood from the heart chambers.

Systolic – measurement of blood pressure taken during systole.

Taper – reduction in training levels to ensure an athlete is fresh for a competitive event.

Tendons – the connective tissue that attach muscles to bone.

Tidal volume – the amount of air that is moved in or out of the lungs in one breath.

Type I fibres – may be termed slow oxidative fibres (SO). They have a lot of mitochondria and oxidative enzymes and a plentiful supply of capillaries. They are well adapted for aerobic respiration.

Type IIB fibres – may be termed fast glycolytic fibres (FG). They are well adapted for anaerobic respiration and reach peak tension very quickly.

Type IIA fibres – fast oxidative glycolytic (FOG) fibres. Similar to fast glycolytic fibres, but with training they are capable of adapting to aerobic respiration.

Veins – carry blood towards the heart.

Vertebrae – the individual bones that make up the spine.

Recommended Reading

Abdominal Training by Christopher M. Norris (A & C Black, London, 1997)

Fitness and Health (Fourth edition) by Brian J. Sharkey (Human Kinetics, Champaigne, Illinois, 1997)

Fitness Programming for the Professional by Fiona Hayes (Summit Training and Education, Hampshire, 1995)

Flexibility for Sport by Bob Smith (Crowood Press, Marlborough, Wiltshire, 1996)

Food for Fitness by Anita Bean (A & C Black, London, 1998)

Program Design for Personal Training by D. S. Brooks (Moves International, Mammoth Lakes, California)

The Complete Guide to Endurance Training by Jon Ackland (A & C Black, London, 1999)

The Complete Guide to Exercise in Water by Debbie Lawrence (A & C Black, London, 1998)

The Complete Guide to Exercise to Music by Debbie Lawrence (A & C Black, London, 1999)

The Complete Guide to Sports Nutrition (Second edition) by Anita Bean (A & C Black, London, 1996)

The Complete Guide to Strength Training by Anita Bean (A & C Black, London, 1997)

The Complete Guide to Stretching by Chris Norris (A & C Black, London, 1999)

Serious Training for Endurance Athletes (Second edition) by Rob Sleamaker and Ray Browning (Human Kinetics, Champaigne, Illinois, 1996)

Sports Nutrition for Women edited by Anita Bean and Peggy Wellington (A & C Black, London, 1995)

Recommended Websites

Balance Fitness Magazine
http://www.hyperlink.com/balance/

Healthnet Jumpsite
http://www.online.edu/health/health.htm

Fitness Sites Jumpsite
http://www.cdc.net/~primus/fpc/
  fpchome.html

Coaching Science Abstracts
http://www.rohan.sdsu.edu/dept/
  coachsci/intro.html

Endurance Training Journal
http://s2.com:80/etj/training/training.html

Swimming Training Journal
http://www.rohan.sdsu.edu/dept/
  coachsci/swimming/index.html

Physician and Sports Medicine
http://www.physsportsmed.com/
  journal.htm

SUMMIT Directions
http://www.the-summit.co.uk

The Southern Traverse
http://www.southerntraverse.com

Gatorade Sports Science
http://www.gssiweb.com/index.html

Institute MAPP
http://www.krs.hia.no/~stephens/
  index.html

The sample programmes in this book were written using Assist Trainer software available from SUMMIT Directions Ltd, 36, Northview Road, Tadley, Hants. UK. http://www.the-summit.co.uk

Useful Addresses

All England Netball Association
Netball House
9 Paynes Park
Hitchin
Hertfordshire SG5 1EH
tel 01462 442344

Amateur Boxing Association of England
Crystal Palace National Sports Centre
London SE19 2BB
tel 0181 778 0251

Amateur Rowing Association
6 Lower Mall
Hammersmith
London W6 9DJ
tel 0181 748 3632

Badminton Association of England
National Badminton Centre
Bradwell Road
Loughton Lodge
Milton Keynes MK8 9LA
tel 01908 268400

British Amateur Gymnastics Association
Lilleshall National Sports Centre
Ford Hall
Lilleshall
Newport
Shropshire TF10 9NB
tel 01952 820330

British Amateur Rugby League Association
West Yorkshire House
4 New North Parade
Huddersfield HD1 5JP
tel 01484 544131

British Canoe Union
John Dudderidge House
Adbolton Lane
West Bridgford
Nottingham NG2 5AS
tel 0115 982 1100

British Cycling Federation
National Cycling Centre
1 Stuart Street
Manchester M11 4DQ
tel 0161 230 2301

British Ski Federation
258 Main Street
East Calder
Livingston
West Lothian EH53 0EE
tel 01506 884343

British Triathlon Association
PO Box 26
Ashby-de-la-Zouch
Leicestershire LE65 2ZR
tel 01530 414234

English Ski Council
Area Library Building
Queensway Mall
The Cornbon
Halesowen
West Midlands B63 4AJ
tel 0121 501 2314

Fitness Professionals
113 London Road
London E13 0DA
tel 0990 133434

Lawn Tennis Association
The Queen's Club
West Kensington
London W14 9EG
tel 0171 381 7000

Midland Counties Athletics Association
Edgbaston House
3 Duchess Place
Hagney Road
Edgbaston
Birmingham B16 8NM
tel 0121 452 1500

Modern Penthathlon Association of Great Britain
Pentathlon House
Baughhurst Road
Baughhurst
Basingstoke
Hampshire RG26 5JS
tel 01734 817181

North England Athletics Association
Suite 106, Emco House
5/7 New York Road
Leeds LS2 7PJ
tel 0113 246 1835

Rugby Football Union
Rugby Road
Twickenham
Middlesex TW1 1DZ
tel 0181 892 8161

South England Athletics Association
Suite 36, City of London Fruit Exchange
Brushfield Street
London E1 6EU
tel 0171 247 2963

Squash Rackets Association
33/34 Warple Way
Acton
London W3 0RQ
tel 0181 746 1616

SUMMIT Directions Ltd
www.the-summit.co.uk

The Exercise Association of England
Unit 4, Angel Gate
City Road
London EC1V 2PT
tel 0171 278 0811

The Football Association
16 Lancaster Gate
London W2 3LW
tel 0171 262 4542

The Hockey Association
The Stadium
Silbury Boulevard
Milton Keynes MK9 1HA
tel 01908 544644

YMCA Fitness Industry Training
112 Great Russell Street
London WC1B 3NQ
tel 0171 343 1850

Index